Angels Are Talking

A Psychic Medium Relays
Messages From the Heavens

By Michelle Whitedove

2010

May God Bless You!

In Love + Light

Michelle Whitedove

Angels Are Talking

A Psychic Medium Relays
Messages From the Heavens

Michelle Whitedove

WHITEDOVE PRESS

In most instances the names have been changed to protect individuals privacy

WHITEDOVE PRESS
PO Box 550966
Fort Lauderdale FL 33355
www.MichelleWhitedove.com

To order additional copies of this book 1-800-444-2524

Book Design & Cover by Gary C. Marshall

Author Photograph by Maliena Slaymaker

Cover Photograph by Maliena Slaymaker

Printed on Acid Free paper / recycled paper
Printed in the U.S.A.

Library of Congress Number 2001097919

ISBN # 0-9714908-0-5 soft cover

ISBN # 0-9714908-1-3 hard cover

First Edition

10 9 8 7 6 5 4 3 2 1

Inspiration

The soft gentle push
From an angels nose,
To help inspire this
Book to flow
Angelic whisper
In your ear,
Will let each ink drop
Release our fear.
Golden hoops, mystical wings
Helped her to write
Of the deeper things
Teachings that open
Doors to our heart
Lighting a pathway
Out from the dark.
Spirit gifted us
With many things
Beautiful auras and magical dreams
Pixies to play with
And sunbeams to chase
Lessons to learn
For every race.
Inspired & guided by
Sweet angel grace,
This book was written
From that magical place

-Maliena Slaymaker

Also by Michelle Whitedove

She Talks with Angels -
A Psychic Medium's Guide into the Spirit World
2000

Angels Are Talking -
A Psychic Medium Relays Messages From the Heavens
2002

Ghost Stalker -
A Psychic Medium visits America's most Haunted Sites
(October 2002)

My Invisible Friends -
A children's book
(December 2002)

Video teaching series:

Creating Your Reality
with Michelle Whitedove

I would like to dedicate this book to the Great Spirit, my Angels, and Spirit Guides, who have once again allowed me to be an instrument for humanity. The love and the guidance that they give me are constant and my source of strength. I am eternally grateful! I would not know how to get through one day without their support.

To Shanté who is my dearest friend in the world and has been a Godsend in helping me to write this book, I could not have done it without her love and support. Most of all I want to thank her for believing in me when no one else would.
I love you.

Special Thanks to Maliena Slaymaker and Mimi Markus for taking time out of their busy lives to help with typing and editing, an arduous process. They were both selfless and thoughtful. I thank you both and I am grateful for your kindness.

CONTENTS

INTRODUCTION

*I*n a dimly lit room, with wooden bookcases covering one wall, candles flicker on a mahogany sideboard table and sacred incense is burning. The glow of an Angel lamp hangs from overhead. Michelle Whitedove sits silently in prayer at an antique desk. Her day begins as usual. The phone rings. Faintly I hear her say, "Hello Tom. Before we start this reading I want you to say a silent prayer with me and give thanks for your Angels and Spirit Guides. Ask them to come forward with information that they would like to share. Also, invite any loved ones who are on the other side to come forward with a message if they have one." As they silently pray in unison, the information begins to flow. The reading begins.

How does one receive such personal information about someone she has never met? "It is a gift and sometimes it is a curse," I have heard Michelle say. Can you imagine the responsibility of being given the most intimate details of someone's life, relaying all types of problems and their solutions? I see how these readings weigh heavy, and they are an overwhelming task at times. But when a heavenly spirit gives news that may be unpleasant, Michelle is also given the correct way to deliver the message with an explanation and a solution. Through her relaying vital information, she is making a difference, one person at a time.

As a psychic, Michelle tunes into the frequency of the person that she is "reading." She has described this to be much like tuning into a radio station. There she is able to receive much information about the person's current life situation, health issues, job skills, finances, romantic interests, family, and she also sees into the person's past.

As a medium, she is able to give closure to so many people that are in a deep state of grief. Contacting a departed loved one is a rare gift that confirms that we really do live forever. Just last week a gentleman came for a second appointment. As he walked into Michelle's office, he greeted her and said, "I want to talk to my wife Carol again!"

Its funny how people perceive her gifts. They think she has a telephone that rings up Heaven. Most people don't realize that loved ones come through when they have a message, not upon demand. Michelle always makes it look easy. She was able to once again reach out to Carol who had recently passed due to brain cancer. Because of the clarity of the first reading, her husband George listened to the tape recorded session over and over again. He was amazed at the detailed information, but most of all it helped heal his broken heart. He knew his wife was no longer in pain and that one day they would be together again.

Readings such as these are invaluable to individuals. But on a larger scale, Michelle's mission is to bring God's message of unconditional love to the public. Organized religion only gives us a fraction of the truth. There is so much more than meets the eye. Gifted "seers" like Michelle are able to converse directly with the other side and relay spiritual knowledge that is to be shared. She answers important questions that many of us ask. What really happens when we die? Are my loved ones okay? What do we do while in heaven? Why am I here? What is the purpose? How can I ease my earthly problems? Most religious leaders can only pass on what they learned during their religious studies or from their interpretation of the scriptures. So, it is wonderful to know that there are modern-day prophets that have the ability to channel information directly from the Heavens just as the ancient prophets of biblical times did. These unique souls have a connection and a personal relationship with the Spirit World. Michelle always says, "God has never stopped talking to us. It is just that some people have forgotten how to listen."

As I have transformed my belief system because of Michelle's personal influence, I know that the information contained within this book will help many more people open themselves up to a larger perception of God, our life on Earth, and our ongoing relationship with the spirit world.

Oceans of Love,
Shanté Powders

I saw them with my bodily eyes as clearly as I see you. And when they departed, I used to weep and wish they would take me with them.

– St. Joan of Arc

WELCOME TO MY WORLD
AN INTRODUCTION

*O*nce again, welcome to my world. I want everyone who reads this book *Angels are Talking* to know that the channeled information contained within is a great gift that God has bestowed upon me. There are many important messages for those who are ready to receive them with an open heart, mind, and spirit.

There is so much to tell, and much more to explain. First and foremost, I want to give you a glimpse into the Spirit World, a place full of wonder and profound knowledge. It is the place that I have always known as my true home. Together we will voyage through the process that we call life and the transition of death. Most importantly, I want to share the knowledge that death is an illusion and that there is much more to our eternal existence than our short experience on Earth. We are powerful beings that create our never-ending journey through free will and through our choices. We affect those on Earth and the beings of the Spirit world. What we do echoes in eternity.

How did I come into this information? As far back as I can remember, even as a small child, I could see, hear and communicate with spirits who I now refer to as my unseen support team, my Guardian Angels, Spirit Guides and loved ones. As a young girl, I assumed that everyone could communicate with spirits. They were my friends and a source of constant companionship since I lacked parental supervision and guidance. I grew up in a home environment void of religion or spirituality. When I was about seven years old, I was drawn to religion. On Sunday mornings, I would jump on a church bus that went through our neighborhood with my best friend Laura, and then we would disembark at a random church. The denomination was unimportant to me I just wanted to worship in God's house. Sometimes this meant that I would travel alone.

So, I chose of my own free will at a very early age, to seek out God and to soak up all that the church could teach me. As a teen, I became a part of one particular religion, but after a few years, I grew disenchanted with the leadership and the judgment that came from my acquaintances in the congregation. With my religious growth, my spiritual gifts also increased. As I looked around in the church, psychically I could see into the souls of those who were teaching me. With disappointment, I saw mostly hypocrites. They were saying the right thing, but when they left the church parking lot, they were living the life of an impostor. As I joined the church of my own free will, I also chose to leave.

I started to experiment with my intuition. When I would ask a question of my unseen support team, I would find that I always had access to an unbelievable source of information. "Ask and the answers shall be given unto you." And I would put the information that I received to the test and it would be so. Honing my intuition, I began to receive information even when I was not asking for it, not only about the people in my life, but also in visions of future events. My relationship with The Great Spirit, my Guardian Angels and Spirit Guides was evolving, and I had learned to trust the information that I was given.

At eighteen, I had a near death experience. What I find fascinating is that it seemed as if I was out of body for hours. What had taken minutes in Earth time was an extended voyage in my lighter body. People think that death is a scary thing, but in reality, it is very peaceful. I was filled with the feeling of unbelievable freedom without limitations and thinking WOW, I look exactly like I did in life only a transparent and more perfect version.

It was quite an occasion. I popped out of my body and was actually hovering above observing, watching and feeling very detached from my physical shell that was being worked on by the paramedics. Eventually, I was pulled away and was drawn into God's white protective light that was so brilliant that I couldn't even set my spirit eyes upon it. There my support team, my Guardian Angels, and my loved ones greeted me. It was then that I was told that I had to go back to my life on Earth.

As we are in life, our same personality shines through in the Spirit World, and I have to say that I put up a heck of an argument, and it was evident that I was not thrilled to go back.

The pure vibration of Heaven is an energy that is not to be forgotten. No, I did not want to go back to my life because the feeling of all encompassing love that pervades the soul is so magical I find it difficult to articulate. I felt love that I had never really felt in a physical body. Ecstasy is the closest word in the English language. In the heavens, there is also instant access to information and knowledge; it felt as if I had downloaded a universal encyclopedia. While in heaven anything and everything that you want to know, all of the information is available for you. So now, you may have in inkling why I wanted to stay.

In my first book, I described my near death experience completely. This was not only to give you confirmation that we do indeed go on to the heavens and that we are never alone, but also because in that experience I received the most wonderful contribution from God. I was reawakened to the importance of my mission and my purpose for coming to Earth. There was a part of me that had forgotten, and I desperately needed to be reminded. For that I am forever grateful. "Spirit" reminds me from time to time, that most people are in a state of amnesia; they have completely forgotten why they are here and what they came to accomplish.

Before I was sent back to Earth, I was given a good look at my future life. I had volunteered for a big mission and was not getting out of it so easily. Some people find the concept hard to grasp, but when one soul is removed from the earthly experience, thousands of souls are affected. How many people will you have come into contact with during your lifetime? In some way, you have affected all of them.

If we will allow it, our free will can intervene with our original contract. My mission is to touch the lives of many people by bringing the message of the Spirit World to the masses. Before coming here, I agreed to be a vessel through which spiritual information would flow. So, I do private counseling sessions to help people individually. Spirit has directed me to write books of channeled information, to teach spiritual development courses, and lecture worldwide. Television and radio are other sources that I utilize to reach millions of people and help to raise the mass consciousness of mankind. I have my hands in a lot of cookie jars.

I don't consider myself special, but I do, however, recognize the information that God and all of my spirit friends have communicated through me is special. As we travel through this book, I will often refer to receiving information from "Spirit." Please know that this is a general term. I am referring to "a spirit source" of the Heavens. Most of the time the information just flows. I do not stop the stream of information and ask that the source be given. It is always of the highest vibration of God, the collective consciousness, the Godhead, Father-Mother-God, Guardian Angels, Spirit Guides, or loved ones. Simply put, I am a light worker, a messenger of God who relays messages from the spirit world to those open to hear them. Each human being contains a great spark of God, and each spark radiates as an inner light that is very unique indeed. I believe that many are called, but few are chosen.

I have been asked if my abilities are a gift or a curse. My abilities are a great gift from God, but they also act as a double-edged sword. I open myself to both the positive and the negative aspects of the human condition. I don't always want to know what people are thinking, especially those people that I love and care about. It is difficult when I see something for a family member, like an issue with their health, an accident or maybe they are just not thinking very kind thoughts about me. It is not always pleasant to know so much. Individuals for the most part are very judgmental, and I hear their thoughts like the waves emitted from a radio station. Sometimes they are crystal clear and a little too loud. When I am out to dinner or at the mall with a friend, I am always flooded with unsolicited facts.

Once, while in an airport during a layover, I was standing in line at a fast food restaurant for a quick bite before my next flight. A middle-aged blond woman with two small children were in the line next to me. I sent a silent prayer into the heavens asking God to bless them with strength and patience in their travels. My heart went out to the mother as she was traveling alone pushing a toddler in a cart with diaper bags, a purse, and carrying an infant. Some mothers should win medals of honor. Waiting for my burger, information about the older child began to stream into my mind. I was being prompted to relay information about the toddler's health problems. Trying to ignore the information, I went to find a seat to hurriedly eat. The health message kept tugging at me, but I did not want to approach a stranger and sound like a rambling lunatic. How would I approach a woman who was not looking for a "psychic" message? Would she hit me or scream for help? I gathered up my nerve, and as she was getting the children prepared to leave the dining area, I stood up and asked if I could have a word with her. Looking startled, she said yes. I introduced myself as a medical intuitive, hoping that it was a term that she might find acceptable. Continuing, I nervously handed her my business card and began to discuss her oldest child's health issues, telling her that her son had severe allergy problems that were affecting his upper respiratory system. Her jaw dropped. I went on to say that he was highly allergic to dairy products, and that if she were to delete them from his diet, he would bounce back to being the picture of health. The lady told me that she had taken her son to several doctors who were unable to solve his on going coughs, runny nose, and ear infections. She smiled and told me that she would remove dairy from her son's diet right away and thanked me for my help.

Although I was not comfortable approaching a stranger at first, I was blessed with a kind woman who was open to some guidance. So just as I was wishing that I could turn off my abilities from hearing the whirling thoughts of the people around me, to the information flooding into my mind, I was able to help one more person.

Obviously, I am much more comfortable relaying messages from my office environment. This is where I conduct private appointments and telephone readings for people all over the world. My assistant is often asked if the information is the same on the telephone as it is in-person. The answer is yes, because there is no limitation of time in distance. "Spirit" has trained me well for my mission. In 1998, I was approached by a local cable TV station that had heard about my abilities and contacted me to see if I was interested in my own program. I agreed because I knew that it would be a wonderful opportunity to get a spiritual message out to the public. Well, it was a LIVE cable television show, and I was extremely anxious when I first started. With no experience and no direction I was on TV. I would choose a topic for every show and then invite callers to ask a personal question on the subject. Soon the phone lines were lit before I was on the air. This was on-the-job spiritual training. I would ask their first name, their birth date, and the specific question. For those of you wondering, no, I am not an astrologer. Your birth date carries a vibration, as does your name. These help me tune into your energy quickly. So, with very little information I was able to relay accurate answers to the callers' questions. Each week I became better and faster. My gifts with time, practice, and experience have become clearer, and I have been able to develop myself to new levels and fine tune my abilities.

This was how my Spirit Guides prepared me for the large number of phone readings that I do today. It is a gift that can be developed. All of my readings are conducted in the same manner. My assistant only takes a first name and a phone number to reconfirm the appointment. No other information is asked for or wanted. For the day of the appointment clients are told to have a written list of questions, so they won't forget important questions that they want answered. Every reading, I start by going into prayer and meditation for my clients. Also, I ask them to pray and invite their Angels, Guides and loved ones to come foreword with any message. Basically, I am just the instrument, the channel to receive whatever information that spirit gives to me past, present, or future. Whether it is a loved one that comes through, insight into a health crisis, or career advice, specific information about the issues that are effecting that person, I touch upon many topics. No two readings are ever the same. It is my job to give them the information unedited from spirit, from my lips to their ears. And spirit will always give specific details; these details are the proof that confirms the accuracy of the information.

When Mr. & Mrs. Bentley came to see me, they had heard of my reputation but were still very skeptical. As they waited impatiently in my office, I could feel an overwhelming amount of grief. I said a silent prayer to help heal their hearts already knowing that they had come hoping to receive some form of communication from a loved one although I did not know who.

As the reading started, spirit told me that it was a male child that the Bentley's wanted to connect with. In an instant, there was a scene unfolding in front of me like a video. It was dusk, and there were a carload of teenagers coming down a wet road in a mountainous area. I could smell the dampness. It was an accident in Europe I said. Your son was with a group of friends. He received trauma to the head and died immediately.

Tears began to flow. The grief of the parents was crushing; all I could feel was their unending pain. The son that they so desperately wanted to connect with was in the room now. My unseen support team and their son were giving the information via pictures, feelings, and even smells.

The Bentley's acknowledged that all of the information that I was receiving was correct, but they were looking for proof that their only child continued to live on in the heavens. They wanted a sign that they could experience themselves to confirm that he was alive and well in the spirit world.

I continued to tell them about their son Joseph, his

outgoing personality, his school, and his hobbies. Joseph told me that he had been around his home looking in on his parents and trying to give them a sign. He plays with the electricity. "Have you noticed?" I asked. Watch. He is trying to give you a sign by the computer. Pay attention and look for it.

There is no greater personal tragedy than the loss of a child. So, I went on to council the parents about their grief. The mother continued to cry. The youthful father had completely shut down. Emotionally he had deadened. He could feel no joy or pleasure. This is not what your son wants. My Guides told me that the father had built a friendship with a boy that he coached in baseball and that this relationship was very positive.

"My son won't be upset will he?" Mr. Bentley asked. No, he only wants you and his mother to move forward and to laugh once again.

As the session ended, I felt disappointed that I could not completely remove their pain and grief, but at least they had some closure and were able to make contact with their beloved son who was on the other side.

Two weeks later Mrs. Bentley called. She was ecstatic! "You'll never believe what has happened," she said. We came home the other day, and there on the computer was our son's password, GODLIKE. No one could have typed it. We were not home and no one knew his password besides the two of us. It was the sign they were looking for, confirmation that their beloved Joseph was still with them and that he was doing fine.

Personally, I find my work very satisfying. When you love something that you do, you will find that you are fulfilling your mission. For those of you that feel that there is something deeply missing in your life, you must open up to new ideas. Some people get caught up in the usual bump and grind of everyday and then get to a point that they ask themselves "Is this all there is?"

I'm here to shout the answer to you, "NO"! There is a lot more to life than what meets the eye. You had a hand in planning this life that you are currently living. Nothing happens because it is an accident; there is a divine purpose and timing for what is happening in your life as you read these very words. So, if you are having an extremely difficult time at this stage in your life, your Spirit Guides and Angels are working overtime to get you to see what you are obviously choosing not to deal with. We all have our contracts that we created, that we agreed to in Heaven with God, which I will cover in the chapter on Spiritual Contracts.

My entire life has been built upon the very foundation that God and his assistants have helped to lie out before me a path, very carefully not one detail forgotten. I try not to look at my life decisions with ego and intellect. For many this might seem shocking. But I listen to the voice of God inside me that is my guide and lights my way, everyday. Wherever that path leads me, it is always for my best interest. There are many doors of opportunities that are disguised. We just need to walk through them. Forget the intellect. What is your gut telling you?

Every time you get those intuitive impressions, whether it is visual in your mind's eye, a knowing, or a feeling, go with it. God and your unseen support team are trying to guide you toward the next phase of your life and your spiritual development. The more that you follow your intuition, the more that you will increase your gifts. The whole trick is learning to decipher the difference between your ego and intellect versus your intuition. The ego would have you think about something, analyze it, and pick it apart where your intuition is a knowing. You feel; therefore, you know. It is the first thing that pops into your head, even when it sounds like a crazy solution. And how you can learn to trust that is every time you get intuitive information, you apply it, you go with it, and you'll see that it is exactly right for you. Maybe it is not for the next person, but for you it's right on target. Then that way you're establishing not only a connection, but also you're having more faith in the information.

God is always talking to us! I am not special. She converses with us all regularly through that little voice in our head, through the dreamtime, signs that she places in front of us, and visions too. Work on fine tuning your intuition, and if you combine it with prayer and meditation, you will very quickly fill up that void within. No amount of chocolate, sex, shopping, drugs, shoes, or fast cars, will make us feel complete. Only our relationship with God and our unseen support make us feel whole.

Someone once asked me, "Don't you ever get lonely?" I replied that the feeling of loneliness is just an illusion. Not one person goes through life alone. I am able to see and converse with the other side. But for many loneliness is their true perception because they feel separate from God. Loneliness is really homesickness; most people miss the connection to heaven and to our Mother-Father-God.

On the average, I have found that people complain of being short of two things that affect their life drastically. One is money and the other is time. When people think of these two separate issues, it always then leads them to the real issue, that of freedom. Money and time equal freedom. I know that the information in the following pages will help you in these areas and others if you will just keep and open mind and spirit. I myself have come to love books for various reasons. Frankly, I love to read and to learn. The most powerful possessions a man can have are those of wisdom and knowledge and the discernment of them, not money, fame, and status like so many people would choose to believe. But wisdom and the discernment of it, this is true power. When our body dies and our soul travels to the other side, it is not the money and material objects that you take with you; it is the knowledge that was gained from your earthly experiences that goes with you.

In this book, I will pass along to you the knowledge and wisdom that has been given to me straight from the heavens. The unchanging truth of God is the only truth that there is, ageless wisdom that is powerful enough to change lives by changing old beliefs. I have come to understand this knowledge as God's Universal Laws. It is the original information before man had twisted the words, hid passages, and misinterpreted God's true message to suit his own needs. These are the same laws that have governed all of the great masters who have walked this Earth. For myself, I believe in making things simple and living a life that is based on these laws without the dogma of man-made religions that create segregation. The truth will set you free. It is priceless, and precious. It is my pleasure to share this journey with each one of you. So, open your hearts, minds, spirit, and even your imagination.

My wish is that people would search for themselves to remember who they really are. Where is it that they came from and where they will return to one day? I wish that mankind will open the lines of communication to others around the planet, and become accepting of those who are different from themselves. It is also my wish that people would communicate more with God and their unseen support team, and pass on this information from generation to generation. Let us learn from our past mistakes not only as individuals, but also as a group. Each individual is important, for in God's eyes we are all equal.

May God Bless You, In Love and Light.
Michelle Whitedove

BUILDING A RELATIONSHIP WITH SPIRIT

*T*here is a great difference between knowing about someone and having a personal relationship with that person. The same is true with GOD.

To have a relationship with God, she does not require you to follow any man made religion. Actually, you will not score any brownie points for choosing to participate nor will you be reprimanded for abstaining from religion. Certainly, I am not of any man-made religion. I like to think of myself as being spiritual. I chose to have a personal relationship with God, which I cultivate on a daily basis. God is my best friend.

Religion was created to give humanity a guideline for living in accordance with the balance of Heaven. The common strand that runs throughout every religion is unconditional love; all of the great masters taught us to love our brother as ourselves. In man's quest for power and control of the people, rules were added that were not directives from above.

Man decided to add "Hell" into the equation for an additional guarantee that humanity would follow the religious regulations as they were put before them all the while, claiming that God authored them. As a malevolent being, God is not judgmental, not jealous, nor would he ever throw us into the pits of hell to burn forever as man's religions would have us to believe.

I define God as everything that there is: as love, as light, as energy, as a Universal consciousness, as you, as me, as my best friend, we are all sparks of God. The Great Spirit created us in his image; we are co-creators like our Mother-Father-God. We inherited a wonderful gift to create through our free will. It is hard for the intellectual mind to grasp exactly all that God is because God is EVERYTHING, masculine, feminine, the universe, the stars, and the ocean. And again, we are limited to what our mind can perceive. Souls that have broadened their knowledge and expanded their belief systems will be able to comprehend these concepts. But even for those more advanced, there is always room to grow. I believe that The Great Spirit resides in other spaces and places as well as in other dimensions like the seven levels of Heaven or the seven states of consciousness. But even in all his glory we can cultivate a personal relationship with our maker.

The first step in having a friendship is to know that God exists and that we are a part of something that is much bigger than ourselves. God has been called by many names: King of Kings, Allah, YAHVEH, Jehovah, Great Spirit, Yahweh, the Creator, Vishnu, Holy Trinity, Cosmic Consciousness, and the list of names goes on and on. Realize that we are always connected to the God consciousness while here on earth. Once we understand that all life has purpose and that most of our experiences especially the painful ones, are needed for the soul's growth to learn and evolve, then we have come to a place of understanding where we can appreciate our life lessons and love God unconditionally.

I want to articulate in words the best I can an analogy to explain our connection to our creator while we are here visiting Earth. Visualize of all of the young adults going off to college. Each day millions of youth say good-bye to their hometown, friends and family and start out on a new adventure, a new stage of life.

All of these students are at school, having separate experiences and learning new skills. Some are freshmen, some are seniors, while others are earning their master's degree. Of their own free will, they come to learn and to be tested in hopes of acquiring a new understanding and a higher education.

After some time away, many become home sick and feel separated by the distance. But these students are still connected to their home by the love in their heart, even when they are miles away and they can't see their family. They are only a phone call away. A loving parent is always eager to hear from his or her child.

There are millions of young adults on college campuses taking new courses at the same time, having different experiences and studying different facets of knowledge. But while these students encounter independent and unique journeys, there is a connection that keeps them attached to their home and families. When students have completed their education, they graduate and prepare for the journey home.

Upon their arrival, they are greeted with a graduation party. With all of their loved ones in attendance, the graduates are congratulated on a job well done.

In this way, our eternal souls are as college students. We willingly leave heaven, our true home, and journey to Earth (college) to learn hard lessons, to pass and fail tests. And then we finally return home to heaven where our spirit family and God reside. Even if we feel we have failed, we are greeted with open arms and are welcomed back home.

No matter how many hard lessons that we learn

and no matter how lonely we get, God is always present. You are connected and never alone. You are only a prayer away; even in the darkest hours when you feel the most abandoned and frightened, you are not alone. God is with you.

*   *   *   *   *

One of the most important beliefs needed in order to have a wonderful relationship with God and our unseen support team (Angels & Guides) is faith, belief in that higher power, faith that we were not just dropped from the sky or that we were born as a baby only to die and that nothing exists after our experiences in this lifetime. Life is a continuation whether it is here on earth or on a different plane of existence. The soul never dies; only the soul's container (the body) does. We chose many vessels to contain our soul during the great span of eternity.

I am not going to debate that the human race came into being due to scientific evolution or that God created us in seven days, the traditional religious belief. I do know that it is not just one of these theories that is accurate, but it is a joining of the two. Evolution and spirituality together complete the puzzle of creation. The point is not that we agree how humans came into being, but more importantly that it is by God's hand that we were created.

Know that in order to have fulfilling friendships, there are two very important ingredients: trust and communication. In order to have a relationship with God and our support team, we must trust them and build a relationship over a period of time. Treat your Creator, Angels and Guides as your very best friends because that is what they truly are. The love that they have for us is always unconditional, regardless of what we do in life. It does not matter whether we think that we deserve such devoted love or not. Their love is not based on conditions. The Great Spirit never leaves us and only wants what is in our best interest.

We are never forced into a relationship. The gift of free will gives us the opportunity to choose what we want to experience during our soul's journey. So, if you want unconditional love and support throughout your life, it is there just by making the effort in maintaining a relationship. Reach out and say "Yes, I can use all the help I can get, assistance in making the best choices in life for myself as well as others around me whom I love." Our spirit helpers hear our thoughts and prayers, more importantly - knows our true intent. We have a choice to work with God and our unseen support team, or we can choose a much more difficult and lonely road. It is up to us individually.

Do you have a best friend? Most people tell their friends just about everything, from the way they feel for someone to their deepest, darkest secrets. Friends share experiences and give advice. Our relationship with the Spirit World is the same. The only difference lies in the fact that God has the best answers and truly cares about you without a motive, just pure unconditional love.

Our souls were created from love. We are love but we can also choose to be other things that are quite the opposite of love. Our free will allows us to experience life lessons and to learn from them. For some people life seems easy, abundance seems to flow for them. For others life is very difficult, always challenging and full of obstacles. I have found that for people who live their lives by the Universal Laws and have a wonderful relationship with the Great Spirit our creator, life is a happier experience for them, rewarding in ways you could not even imagine.

So work on building a relationship with Spirit. Talk to them whether you speak out-loud or silently. Prayer is a powerful tool. Prayer is the act of talking to God, when you voice your thoughts, goals and dreams.

Know what you want and give thanks for those aspirations made manifest. But realize there is a difference between what we want and what we need. When you are going to pray for something, ask yourself,

"What is truly in the best interest for all concerned?" And know that your intent (or motivation) plays a great role in whatever you do. Your motives will be a determining factor in the outcome of your prayers.

A prayer should come from love, faith, and gratitude. There is a more productive way to pray. If a mother is praying for her child's well being with fear in her heart, what is the feeling, the intent that is being sent into the universe? How much more effective is the prayer that is said by the parent with a glad heart, with faith and gratitude? What outcome is each parent preparing for? Give this some thought and retrain yourself to pray in a positive manner. You will see a difference in the outcomes.

Communing with God has been practiced by every religion since the beginning of time. Meditation and prayer are time-tested methods that allow each human to connect directly to the God consciousness.

It is equally important that you listen. For thousands of years Eastern religions have practiced the art of mediation. For those who are unfamiliar with the practice, it may look strange, especially when first viewed from a Christian background. Chanting, humming or sitting in a lotus position are formal procedures adopted by some to facilitate the meditation process. Meditation is simply the art of tuning out the world and tuning into to God.

Meditation is only one method of listening to God and your spirit helpers. Meditation is learning to quiet the mind to listen to the guidance that is being given to you through your higher consciousness or intuition. In this way, you receive valid information without ego from your lower self. Some people call this quiet voice within intuition.

I prefer to listen to that voice for guidance because I know that my intuition is God talking to me. That gut feeling is telling me maybe I should do things differently. It's a suggestion, a spark of inspiration. Unfortunately, I have learned the hard way that when I don't listen to that inner guidance, I am sorry later. Our initial instincts are more often correct than not.

Meditation is a tool that each human being can use to connect directly to the Spirit World. Your higher self is the part of your soul that is always linked to God, Guardian Angels, Spirit Guides, and the universal consciousness. Opening communication through meditation not only raises your vibration, but can ultimately grant you the ability to access ALL information, past, present, and future. In this way when frequently used, meditation increases your psychic abilities, and you will begin to consciously know the difference between the ego, from one's lower self and the intuition, or one's higher self. Meditation in combination with fasting is a highly useful tool that heightens spiritual awareness.

Some religions would have us believe that only the highest-ranking officials in the church can converse with God, but this is untrue. In fact, most of the time it is the complete opposite. It is the humble and unassuming that is truly closer.

There are many forms or ways of meditating. Breath is the gift of life, and it is the instrument used by all who meditate. There are many methods of meditation. Be assured there is not a correct way. There are many roads that lead to the same destination. Your job is to find the right path for you!

Do you feel more at ease lighting candles and sitting in a lotus position while listening to soft music? Some people prefer to lie down in the dark at night before going to sleep and have complete quiet while doing deep breathing exercises to achieve this state. Personally, I can meditate in a matter of minutes to achieve this higher state of awareness due to years of practice. I found that each person in time finds what works best for him or her and that will become his or her style or choice of meditation. The more you practice, the better you become in achieving this heightened state of awareness; however, it does take time, so don't become discouraged so quickly.

For beginners it is very normal to find meditation difficult because the mind is full of chatter. But the more you fight the thoughts that are streaming through your mind, the more they will persist. The best council I can give you is don't fight it; just let the thoughts flow without focusing on them. Relax the body and concentrate on your breath until you reach a place of quiet and peace. Breathe deeply through the nose; then exhale through the mouth. Listen to the rise and fall of your breath. Feel the body fill with oxygen. The purpose for this technique is to give the mind something to do by focusing on relaxing and breathing.

How will you know that you are achieving this goal of quiet and peace through meditation? One way to sense this occurring is when you lose track of time; for example, you think it has been 15 minutes, and it's been more than an hour. Another way to tell you are achieving the goal is that you get so relaxed that you go to sleep, especially if you have difficulty sleeping.

The greatest gift of meditation is connecting to God and all your helpers as well as raising your vibration to the frequency of unconditional love.

How else does God communicate with us besides meditation and intuition? Spirit communicates through synchronicities, signs and our dreams.

When a person goes to sleep, it is not just the physical body that is resting, but also the ego or lower consciousness. In the deep stages of sleep, your soul is set free from the physical limitations of the body to travel into the Spirit World where you can connect to the heavens, God, loved ones, and your support team. Whether you remember or not, everyone dreams. The dream world is a doorway to the other side. Our soul moves through the veil of illusion of earthly life so that we are free to reach God and the Spirit World. Dreaming is a very important tool that we as humans have to connect directly to God. It is also the easiest way for our guides and Angels to connect to us even if we don't remember consciously. So pay attention to your dreams and astral journeys, for there is important information contained within your out-of-body experiences.

Synchronicities are what some people call coincidences. But the word coincidence infers that there are random events taking place. But let me correct this misnomer. There are no coincidences that take place in our universe. Everything happens for a reason. Synchronicities are messages or signs that we need to take seriously. They are synchronized events that play themselves out in front of us for a purpose. They have meaning. So, the next time you hear yourself say, "What a coincidence!" review the event and try to see the message. Is it a warning? Is it an opportunity or just information to use in the future? The Spirit World is always talking to us and giving us signs to show us what we need to see.

If you feel that you are having a difficult time in connecting to God and your helpers, ask for a sign or confirmation. Tell them to turn up the volume so to speak, and believe me they will. Their purpose is to serve you at your will. Do not let self-made limitations or beliefs get in the way of this divine gift that God has bestowed. Everything is possible! Do you want to have a happier and healthier life that is joyful, a life with less pain, fear, and grief? I know I do!

Your fear can stop you from making the conscious connection to God and your support team. Fear will paralyze you and prevent you from making any progress spiritually or even in life. Fear will stop you dead in your tracks. God and Spirit know your fears, and they do not wish to scare you in any way, not even in the slightest bit. So, they are very careful not to give you more than you can handle. For example, if an Angel was to show herself to you during the night at the side of your bed and you awoke to see this glowing supernatural being, most people would have a heart attack, even if you had asked your Angel to appear. This is why our Angels and Spirit Guides usually give us signs and confirmations that we can accept. Gradually these signs will be become bolder as we open ourselves to receiving spiritual information. It is never their desire to frighten you because they know that you would just shut yourself off to any other experiences. Our unseen support team knows what you can handle even if you disagree.

In order to have a relationship with God all we need to do is ask and then it is simply a matter of going through the motions. Go through the steps like we would in having a friendship with anyone that we choose to let into our life and love. It is important to be grateful for that person always and give thanks, have gratitude in our hearts for such a wonderful relationship. Trust and communicate. Know that it takes two people to have a successful union of love. You have to be a friend to someone in order to have a true friendship!

Don't forget to listen, and whenever in doubt, ask. Never assume. It is a give and take. What we put into a friendship or any kind of relationship is what we will get back in return. The energies and efforts put forth are greatly rewarded in regards to God and all her many helpers.

The Creator has given us the Universal Laws as a blueprint to help guide us through life. The laws do not change with the times as religions do. I like to pattern my life by these laws that I wrote about and addressed in my first book *She Talks with Angels*. They are simple and uncomplicated strategies for success, suggestions from God to help mankind. The law of unconditional love is the basic foundation. If we would all just live life by this one simple rule, our world would change overnight. The law of karma is what comes around goes around. For our every word, thought, or deed there is a reaction or consequence that comes back to us.

Consciously working with these two laws alone will alter the course of our life. Monitoring our thoughts is a good way to keep ourselves in check. Are we thinking loving thoughts towards those that we interact with on a daily basis? Are we going out of our way to help those in need? Are we praying for the world? Remember, we are co-creators with God. We have to ask ourselves, "What am I creating?"

I try to live my everyday life in my higher state of mind in the state of grace, gratitude, and come from love in all that I do. I have never said this is an easy thing to do. It is a challenge. It seems as if someone is always trying to push your buttons. But you feel so much better when you release your attachments and expectations from outcomes.

If you really want to make your life more fulfilling and successful, then do this. Build a friendship with God, your Spirit Guides, Guardian Angels, and treat your fellow man with love. I assure you that life will be much more fulfilling.

*To pretend angels do not exist
because they are invisible
is to believe we never sleep
because we don't see
ourselves sleeping.*

– Saint Thomas Aquinas

GUARDIAN ANGELS & SPIRIT GUIDES

eople often ask me if Angels and Spirit Guides are one in the same? There is a difference between the two, but they both have a very similar purpose, which is to assist people on Earth with their spiritual mission. They work in perfect harmony with each other recognizing that they are equal. As a team, they are assigned to work and to serve a specific human being. When put together Guardian Angels and Spirit Guides create a wonderful support group for each of us because they only have our best interest in mind. Each of their energies is slightly different because of the vibration or frequency of their spirits, yet when they are together, they achieve a harmonious balance. God's wisdom never ceases to amaze me. She knows exactly what her children need to accompany them through life, which is the combination of these spirits that love each of us unconditionally. Quietly, our support group works primarily behind the scenes. The main reason for this is that they do not want to frighten us because most humans are fearful of what they do not see or understand. When we are fearful, we are sending a message to the universe that says, "We doubt. We do not believe in the power of God." Our Guardian Angels and Spirit Guides are invisible to most people because they are in a different dimension or realm, which is outside of time and space as we know it.

Our unseen support team eagerly waits to assist us in any way possible, but many times, unknowingly, we sabotage their ability to help us. They must honor our "free will" because it is one of God's Universal laws that all beings must abide by. Our free will gives us the opportunity to create any future that we want to experience. Angels and Guides can send us signs, but our actions, thoughts, and deeds ultimately create our experiences. We can interfere with our helpers by choosing not to be open minded enough to pay attention to their signs and messages that they are giving to us. We allow our intellect and ego to get in the way, and we do not listen to their advice. They cannot force us do anything against our own free will, nor can they intervene in a way that contradicts our wishes. Angels and Guides must be invited to effect change in our lives.

Another way that we make their job very difficult

is by telling God and our Angels how to fix our problems. For those people that have faith in God and believe in prayer, many times they will appeal to God and ask for what they think is the solution to their problems. In this way we limit ourselves and interfere with their divine wisdom. The result is that we block the best solution for our problem, the answer to our prayers. I have come to know by my own experience through prayer and the information that has been given to me by the universal consciousness that the best thing each person can do is to "let go and let God." This means that "spirit" knows what is in our best interest and for our highest good. What we need and what we want are usually entirely two different things.

When I'm in prayer, I give thanks for what I want and I have faith that it is already done in that moment. I claim it and only have gratitude in my heart. I know that God's will is always the correct outcome for myself. I am very specific in my requests and have a pure intent while praying; therefore God knows what I need, feel, and want. But ultimately the solution to my problem is in his hands. I think it is presumptuous of us to tell God and our support team how, what, and when to do their job. I trust they know best. How could we possibly know the answers in the first place? If we did, we would not need anything and all would be perfect from the start. There would be no need to incarnate on Earth; there would be neither karma nor lessons to experience.

The Angel kingdom is made up of light beings that God created to serve humanity. Angels are of the purest energy; their very essence is love and light. They have a very high frequency, one of the highest vibrations of God's children because they are made of unconditional love. They vibrate so high their powerful energy could literally blow us away. This is one of the reasons that physical manifestations are not so common. It is not often that our Guardian Angels reveal their true form to us. When they do take on their lighter bodies and appear before us, it is a blessing from God. They must lower their vibration, and we, as humans, must raise ours. The Angel kingdom is a large part of the universal consciousness. They only know one way of being, and that is doing the will of God while coming from unconditional love. Angels do not experience the duality of Earth because they do not have free will like we do. Some religious groups argue that Angels do have free will. My answer is this: if an Angel automatically chooses the highest and best solution, God's will, then this is not free will because there is no choice to be made. Angels always do God's will. There is only one way.

Angels are a different group of Gods children. They were created before humans to serve God and to give glory to him. The Angel kingdom does not have the same experiences that humans find so necessary. Our Guardian Angels do not go through the process of reincarnation; it is not needed because they never experience themselves as separate from God. As humans, we think of our being a fragment or a piece of the puzzle yet separate from the whole. Humans wait for their return to heaven to fit that piece back with the other pieces of the puzzle so that it is now complete. Yet, we are never separate from God or alone. Angels do not experience themselves as individuals; they accept and know that their energy is a part of the collective consciousness. Angels are selfless without ego. All of the spirits that make up the Angel kingdom are devoted to doing God's work. They are his messengers and helpers that are constantly singing praise to God. The Angel family has a perfect order and balance to all that they do.

Guardian Angels

Two Guardian Angels are assigned to each human to assist us through the duration of our earthly life. God loves us so much that she assigns these

Angels to us before we are even born to protect, heal and guide us. Our Guardian Angels help to assist in our birth as we come into being as humans on Earth, and they guide us through the transition we know as physical death. Theses Angels are limitless and can do anything with God's approval. They will ask permission to intervene on our behalf. They petition God for us.

People often ask me what they look like. Our Guardian Angels will choose one gender for our benefit and understanding, one that we can relate to better. What is the sex of our Guardian Angels? Most people will have both a female and a male Guardian Angels. The sex is whatever you are more comfortable with and need. But know this: Angels are not limited to gender: humans get so hung up on what color they are, their looks and their sex. The angel kingdom is so above and beyond the limitations of physical form and ego. They can choose to be male or female depending on what we need. But they can also take on their more natural androgynous form. Angels are truly genderless. I want to convey that Angels do not come across with a great deal of individual personality. They are more nebulas. Some Angels have wings, but more often, I find they do not. It is the Archangels that have very grand beautiful, white wings, like the Archangel Gabriel. Many of the Earth Angels have wings too, but they are slightly different. Their wings are smaller and could be compared more to a butterfly's wings. Our Guardian Angels usually do not have wings. I have found all Angels, regardless of their position or title, are the most breath taking with their appearance and aura. All Angels seem to have been cut from the same cloth because they emanate the same energy. This energy that they radiate is love that causes instantaneous healings in many cases because of their pure love for humanity. Guardian Angels help to heal us in many different areas: the physical body, the emotions, and the astral body. Most of the Angels that I have witnessed are guardians who are dressed in a flowing type of light colored simple robe or gown. The most unusual aspect of them is the color of their eyes. They are a color that I have yet to see on Earth. Their eyes are a combination of a radiant bluish purple color. These striking eyes are the first things that you notice about their physical appearance, but their pulsating aura, which is their energy field, is seen and felt. Long after your Guardian Angel has left the room, you will still see and feel its glowing energy field. The colors in their auras are usually vivid gold, shades of yellow and white. The iridescent white will often shift to silver with hues of gray. For me, the most common color that I have witnessed time and time again is shades of gold. I have seen other colors in the energy field of Angels as well. Some Guardian Angels will have pinks and purples in their aura. The color is a vibration and dependent on the Angel's mission and purpose. Our Guardian Angel's aura has a size and shape just like a human's aura which also has an electro-magnetic field. However, angelic auras, are bigger, and they glow much brighter. They are overflowing with love and energy. Words cannot describe the magnificence of it. Artwork through the ages has depicted Angels with halos. Angels were painted with wings and halos in a great deal of the artwork from the medieval and the renaissance periods. Some of the greatest artists ever known, painted angels with transparent halos above their heads. This was their interpretation of what the artist was seeing and trying to relay to admirers. What the artists saw was the light right above the Angel's head, referred to as the crown chakra. Gold was the color emanating the strongest from this area. It gives the appearance of a halo, but it is actually the Angel's aura that pulsates the strongest from this point above its head.

I would like to share with you an experience that I had with my Guardian Angel. I was outside in front of my office in the early evening saying goodbye to a client while engaged in a brief conversation, when a light and energy caught my eye and pulled me towards the spirit. As I looked closely, my Angel started to take form in her lighter body where I could make out the details of what she looked liked. My Guardian Angel's lighter body was like the transparent form of a holographic image, three-dimensional and physically perfect. Every feature was beautiful to say the least. She had a mix of golden blond to strawberry hair, very pale complexion, ivory skin tone, and those deep blue-purple eyes that penetrate you to your very soul. She was wearing a floor length ivory lace gown, and her hands and fingers were long and graceful. She was human height with a slight medium build. Her aura was multi-colored; it emanated and hovered all around her. It was like watching a rainbow dance, the primary color being gold. She stood still long enough to make sure I got a good look at her as she smiled at me. She communicated to me with her soul to my mind, telepathically. It was a mixture of feelings and pictures. I was hearing her voice in my head through clairaudience. She was conveying to me how much she loved me and that she was constantly by my side, supporting me through a difficult time in my life. She gifted me with this sign and confirmation to encourage me when I needed her most. She assured me that everything was going to be all right and that I should listen carefully to her guidance. The next thing I knew, her energy started to break up. It was so amazing. Her essence turned to twinkling gold dust, and very dramatically, the tiny little gold lights shimmered from the sky down. Before hitting the ground, the gold dust disappeared. It all happened so fast that my client thought I had seen a ghost by the expression on my face. I asked my client, "Didn't you see that?" She didn't see a thing, but she knew I definitely saw something. It was almost unreal or I should say surreal. It's nice to know that we are not alone and she knew that I needed a visit, which would always be a reminder to me of her love and support.

Spirit Guides

Spirit Guides are like our best friends in the entire world except they are on the other side of the curtain or veil looking out for each of us with only our best interest at heart. I have always said they make better friends than the friends we have in life here on Earth. Our Spirit Guides reside in the same place as our Angels, in heaven, which is outside of this Earth realm. The advantage of having them is that they are loyal and aid us not only for the duration of our life here, but also in the after life. Yet, our Spirit Guides never fail us and are always there especially in great times of crisis. Actually, this is the time when they are working over time and their hardest to get us to see what it is that we need to do. When we are not living our life according to our spiritual blueprint, they will direct us towards the changes that need to be made. When we find ourselves at one of the worst places in life, we have to stop and ask ourselves the tough questions. Why is this happening? What issues of mine do I need to look at? How can I make corrections in my life, so I will not repeat this situation again? Our guides cannot force us do anything, but they can make us uncomfortable. They are the beings that are certain and constant in our life. They love us unconditionally and accept us with our imperfections and never complain. They always listen and can relate to our earthly problems because they have incarnated before here on this earth and have experienced many life lessons. Pain and suffering is something that they understand. They have experienced joy and happiness too. This is why we need their assistance because they are familiar with the trials and tribulations that we go through, and they know how challenging it is for each individual.

Each human contains a spark of God's light. A fragment of God resides inside of each of us. As our soul travels to other realms, one Spirit Guide is appointed to travel with us and many times will continue to be our teacher in between lives or incarnations. God has assigned this spirit helper that is usually an advanced teacher or Master Guide on the other side. It is common that we will have the same Spirit Guide through many incarnations. In this way, we will be very well acquainted with our helper. We have been repeating this process of reincarnation over and over for a very long time. I call them "Good Old Faithful" because they know us well and want to support us. Usually our Spirit Guide is our main spirit helper that works very closely with us. They are familiar and understand our weaknesses and strengths. Most of the time, they understand our hearts better than we do. Guides are well acquainted with our purpose in life, our karma, spiritual contracts, and our entire blueprint. They have been trained and prepared to take on this task that is very serious to them. These spirit helpers want us to do the best we can here on Earth to complete our mission because if we fail or do poorly, they will reflect upon this and feel that they have failed us in some way or that they could have done a better job. Much like a parent with a child, the relationship is somewhat similar. Our Spirit Guides are trained in a particular area where they usually specialize and will primarily work with us in that area. For example, if you are a writer, teacher and lecturer, your career would be in an area of education, and your Spirit Guide would also be a teacher. The Spirit Guide would highly influence your energy, especially in its area of expertise. Much more inspiration comes from them than you can imagine.

These Spirit Guides have a vocational aspect and are chosen to help us in that specific way. Every human has at least one Spirit Guide at minimum, but you are not limited to just one helper through the duration of your life. We can draw more Guides and Angels to ourselves, particularly as we advance spiritually. Sometimes these advanced beings will choose us because they are attracted to our light and mission and feel they can aid. I often refer to some guides as part-time, because they are assigned to us at a certain time in our life briefly due to a crisis or problem we might be having. They are there to help us fix it. Then they move on. These part-time guides come to serve us for the length of time that is needed. The number of spirit guides can vary, but we always have at least one.

Our Spirit Guides are much different than our Guardian Angels, yet they have one thing in common that never changes; they are always helping us! Spirit Guides are very different from our Guardian Angels for several reasons. One reason is they have an individual personality and energy that has a completely different vibration. In comparison, I have found while working with guides that they are much more talkative and easier to make contact with because of their lower frequency. Spirit Guides are much more expressive about the information that they bring across whether it is for us or about themselves. They seem to experience themselves more as individuals and eagerly give their name, describe their appearance and their job to help us to better understand their role. It also benefits us to get familiar with their energy and work with them. Our Spirit Guides are souls that have lived here on Earth before and have chosen of his or her own free will to work with humans. All of the Spirit Guides are just like us with the exception that they no longer need to incarnate, and they have reached a higher state of consciousness. In the next dimension, they are teachers, guides and helpers to humanity. Spirit Guides have titles, and there is a perfect order to how they work. Some guides have been working longer in this field and are more experienced. Younger Spirit Guides have a teacher above them to assist them as well. They have different levels or ranks; for example, a Master Spirit Guide is one of the highest-ranking titles or positions to have. This title has to be earned, of course, and that is a soul that is very highly developed and close to God. The Master Guides usually serve to assist and teach other Spirit Guides that are not as experienced.

For instance, here is a situation which might be challenging for a beginning Spirit Guide who lacks experience. A person is having a difficult time here on Earth in every aspect; his life is a mess, and he feels like giving up and taking his life. If this person's Spirit Guide does not know how to handle the human's desire to take his own life, then the Spirit Guide goes to heaven to receive guidance from the Council and its teacher as what it is to do. Through the Council, not only is the Spirit Guide assisted, but so is their charge. Scenarios such as this play out every day here on Earth. Usually, our Guides and the Council have the ability to console the person and give him hope or a solution. But the final outcome is ultimately up to the individual. Our free will can override any assistance that has been offered. Guides can do as much as we will allow them to, but because of man's ignorance, we don't always choose the best solution.

Currently I have a Native American Guide named "Wolf Man." This is a name that I gave him that just stuck after a while. It started out as a joke because he would always come to me as a wolf and then turn into a man. It works for both of us; guides usually just want us to be comfortable with them. Humor is a great tool to lighten things up a bit and make it easier. "Wolf Man" is a warrior and a medicine man. He is very strong and quite firm with his guidance with me. This is the physical form he takes, and his energy is exactly what I need, or it would not be given to me in that manner.

One night he came to me through a dream and was giving me a warning that I could not interpret. He was very persistent and actually scared me a little bit. As I awoke in the middle of the night, I was agitated because he was so aggressive; I misunderstood and thought he was being too pushy. That morning I awoke with the feeling that something really awful was about to happen, like a death or accident in the family. I even went as far to express this to my household. I was so high strung that I wanted to jump out of my body and became shaken and ill. I went back to the visions that my guide gave me; he was very visual with his information. He even went as far as to show me a picture of his face up close. He took his knife and cut his face like a slash with an open flesh wound. Now you can understand why I thought he went a little too far. I shared this information with my family but still didn't understand the meaning. In a matter of minutes, in front of our house, my oldest son had a severe accident while attempting a new trick while jumping a ramp on his bicycle. Without wearing a helmet, he flew off the bike in mid air, landing face first on the asphalt. He took the blunt of the fall on his face, and it was a horrific shock for a mother to see. He lay in the front yard as we were waiting for the ambulance; his front teeth were knocked out, his jaw broken. His lip was completely severed, and part of it stuck to his braces. His mouth was a bloody gaping wound. The paramedic said that his nose was broken, and they thought he might have injured his spine and fractured his wrist.

Of course, Wolf Man's visions made sense now, but it was too late. My guide had been trying to warn me, so hopefully, I could have prevented it from happening. It made sense, but now I needed my unseen support team's help more than ever. I prayed all the way to the hospital. Asking for the assistance of my son's Angels and Guides, I also called upon Rafael the Archangel of healing.

The accident that could have been so much

worse was lessened by the intervention of God, Rafael, my son's and my support team. The list of possible injuries that the emergency room attendants gave me was incorrect. Nothing was broken or fractured. We spent a few days in the hospital as his face healed and teeth were saved. He didn't even need plastic surgery. I know that my prayers were answered. By looking at my son, you would have never known that he had a traumatic accident. This is a perfect example of the difference that prayer, faith, and working with "spirit" can make. I am very grateful for the immediate healing, and I'm also glad I have a very persistent Spirit Guide.

In this way, you, too, can call on your support team in the time of an emergency. They are always on stand-by just waiting to be asked for assistance. I assure you that your emergency will be lessened.

Spirit Guides may have an ethnic look, individual personalities, and unique names. They specialize in different work areas and in their healing techniques. Their missions are not all the same; much depends on the human that they are working with. Spirit Guides are very much like us with human characteristics, but they are on the other side watching our backs to protect us. Some guides are quiet and reserved; some are very forward and strong. They are all very unique and special in their own right.

Our Guardian Angels and Spirit Guides will interact with us in anyway that we are open to receive their help though the dream-time is the easiest way for them to communicate and visit us. Through meditation and prayer, we can actively work together consciously. It's important that each of us make an effort to use these tools to converse with our helpers. The dream-time is an automatic doorway for our Angels, Spirit Guides and loved ones to come through and visit us. We receive premonitions, answers to our problems and visits from loved ones as well as our support group. When we meet up with our helpers in the spirit world, it is a great deal easier for them versus when they try to make contact with us during our daily lives with so many distractions. We are able to receive and understand the information that is passed to us in the dream state easier. Let's not forget to pay attention to the doorway to this spirit world each night or when we lay sleeping. Our dreams are actual events and detailed information that is being shown to us. If we are not clear on the information that is being given, we can ask for our Spirit Guide to reveal it to us in another way we would understand. We can thank them for a sign or message that is quite clear. Don't be afraid to ask your helpers to turn it up, the volume that is. They enjoy when we are making the effort to work with them because our effort is showing them not only that we care, but that we are learning and of our own free will evolving. Our spirit helpers can be very loud and clear in their communication when we do not have fear and allow them to come forward. Remember, they would never hurt you.

Meditation gives us the opportunity to take time out of our active lives to reach out to those in the spirit world to make contact with them. We are making the effort for a change, going within to find the answers instead of looking outside of ourselves. Some people will meditate on the problem that they are having, hoping to be given some clear guidance or the solution that is needed. Another technique that is more popular is to quietly go into a meditative state, being open to receive whatever guidance is given from spirit. When we meditate, we are listening to spirit, giving them a chance to speak and communicate with us. Meditation raises our vibration and is the best way to increase our own intuitive abilities.

Intuition is the voice of our higher self or God part self, talking to our lower mind's ego. Intuition advises us of what is in our best interest and is the way that our Guardian Angels and Spirit Guides communicate with each of us. The intuition is also referred to as our gut feeling, our instincts, or sixth sense. It is a knowingness based on our feelings. Intuition is a part of every human being, but I have found that some people's psychic feelings or impressions are at different levels. Some people are much more developed in this area. Practice makes perfect. The more you go with your gut feeling or what you think is just a hunch, the more that you are trusting and building this connection with your Angels and guides. We have to learn to hear that little voice inside ourselves and be able to decide with clarity if that voice was our intellect/ego or our intuition speaking to us. I always say that intuition is usually the first impression or feeling we get in any given situation in which we feel a clarity and knowing. When the ego and intellect take over by rationalizing and thinking things over to reach a conclusion, we become more confused.

Prayer is the way we each individually have a conversation with God and our support team in spirit. We express ourselves and give thanks to God. Communication is one of the most important ingredients in having a relationship with anyone but especially with God. The spirit world always hears our prayers and is eager to answer them. Our faith and sincerity is what will determine the results of our prayers. We need to consider how to articulate our thoughts into words because God is quite literal. Be careful what you ask for because you will get exactly that. Prayers should be used as a direct link to God to give thanks, not just to ask for what we think we need. Prayer is a combination of the human's will and the word combined to create the desired outcome, the manifestation of one's desires if done with a pure intent. When we take time out of our day and specifically dedicate that time to communing with God, then we are not only improving our life, but we are able to have a positive effect on the world. We have to develop and work with all of the tools that are presented to us in order to improve our relationship with our Angels and Spirit Guides. Meditation, prayer, dreams, and our intuition are the tools that each of us has. How we choose to use these tools is entirely up to each of us.

* * * * *

Seven Levels of Heaven
Where do our Angels, guides and loved ones reside? There are some mysteries that are not meant

to be solved while our soul is in its earthy container. But during my channeling sessions, I poke and prod, always trying to glean more information about the Heavens and what goes on in the spirit world. I have a complete remembrance of some information, and other knowledge I am constantly piecing together.

In heaven, there are seven levels. An Archangel governs each level, and each Archangel oversees legions of Angels that are there to assist the Archangels with various aspects of that particular level. The Archangels have a specific position with special tasks to fulfill. It is their job to assist and serve the creator and help to keep perfect order as well as balance to the heavens. The Archangels are in charge of attending to the human race and the planet as well.

The heavens are a vast place and we relate to this space by its levels of light and variations of energy vibrations. It is divided into levels. Souls will reside on different levels determined by the collective group consciousness and their stage of evolution. These souls will reveal their maturity by the colors of their energy which states who they are and how experienced they are. Our soul's colors tell a story of our journeys and experiences. We are known for our colors. This states our ranking and title. Everything about us is revealed in our energy and its color, which has a vibration as well as size. Our ranking is another way that we recognize our loved ones and family in the heavens. Most of us have had many incarnations and choose these journeys at different times as well as places. We will not always recognize a particular face or body for this reason, but we do know each other by the soul's energy and light. We all have had different faces and various shells to contain the soul. I think of them much like masks or costumes that we wear for a while. We understand and relate also to these various levels by the different groups of souls with their colors that state their development.

The beginner or baby souls and young souls are on the lower levels of heaven. We recognize them by their white auras, which tell us that they are young. The shades of blue are colors that belong to the more experienced souls that are at a faster level of learning. I consider these souls to be in the middle of their development. The purple colors will have shades and variations that we have not even seen on earth. The old souls to very wise master souls are in that color ranking and reside in the mid to upper levels of Heaven. Each soul will evolve through every shade and variation of colors whether it is white, blue or purple.

The gold tones and silver are usually associated with the angel kingdom and the Council. Only highly advanced beings are associated and recognized by the gold and silver colors that reside in the upper levels of Heaven.

As we get closer to the seventh level of Heaven, which is the Godhead, we will experience the pure light of God. As we go higher, this light will become brighter and intense. As we journey closer to the godhead, the light is overwhelming and has the highest amount of concentrated energy of unconditional love. The knowledge and wisdom of who we are in relation to God is limitless and mind boggling to us humans. Souls that work their way to the seventh level will no longer feel or experience the separateness of God on any level. We come into the full awareness of who we are and that we are not a fragment of the collective consciousness. Our energy will return to the Godhead, the whole. We will not experience any separateness as we become one with God. Our individual energy combines to join with the Universal Consciousness. We become part of God, the oneness of all that is.

The levels of heaven consist more of soul groups that represent the working order and awareness of that place. The lower levels of heaven, one, two, and three, are usually reserved for the healing spaces that are needed more for the younger souls. The places that souls choose to rest and contemplate their life is usually in a space like paradise or utopia. This level is the place that reflects a perfect version of Earth. The animal kingdom and nature are the energies that make up paradise. The spirit of every animal that has ever existed resides here; dinosaurs, the wooly mammoth and every other species past, present, and future, all dwell in harmony. There are also animals and colors that we haven't even seen on Earth. The fairy kingdom and Earth Angels such as cherubs reside on this level of heaven too. These are all a different group of God's children. Many human souls choose this level for healing because it is peaceful, and it reminds them of Earth. In this place they are immersed in an amazing scene of nature's bounty while healing on this level.

Another lower level is the place that all souls will journey to frequently because there the elders work and the hall of records exists. On this level each soul will experience its life review before the council. Whether we are just coming out of a life or getting ready to choose a life to incarnate, this is a place where we are guided and counseled in our endeavors. Between lives, we will visit the hall of records and review our past lives to try to study and learn from our earthly experiences. The hall of records is an active place where we can find a great source of knowledge.

The middle level of heaven begins at the end of the third level and goes into the fourth and fifth. On the middle levels some healing still occurs, and this level supplies the places to do it. I find the middle levels to be occupied by older souls living out their experiences in heaven because it is perfect and beautiful. Some souls choose to live and evolve at this level. Quite frankly, it is easier for them to progress in this place than to reincarnate on Earth where it is harsh and take the risk of creating more negative karma. They choose not to incarnate anymore. It is usually not needed for these older souls' growth unless they just want to incarnate to volunteer and serve humanity out of love and compassion. They set up communities to live in and pick the groups of other soul clans that they will interact with. They often will create beautiful homes to live in this environment. Life goes on regardless of whether we are here on earth as humans or in the heavens living a full life. Some souls will choose to incarnate on different stars or planets. We have many different spaces and places where energy lives. We are multi-dimensional beings and our energy is not limited to being contained just in one world. Spirit Guides also reside on these mid-levels. Younger Spirit Guides and teachers will educate the souls that wish to be helpers to humanity and other human souls. There is a school that is on this level to help train and teach skills that are needed to be a Spirit Guide. Guides also help to teach the souls that are on these levels and are living out their existence in the heavens but still need love, guidance, and support. These souls still have lessons and experiences to learn from in order to grow and evolve to a higher level.

The sixth and seventh levels of heaven are the most evolved and highest levels of love. It is the brightest of all levels and represents the love vibration completely. On the sixth and seventh levels only the most advanced beings reside. The Master Spirit Guides, Angels, and teachers live on the sixth level. They are the closet to the universal consciousness and help to represent that to all other life by example. Of course, this is quite an accomplishment for souls to get to this level of wisdom and knowledge. Only the most evolved souls can handle this intense energy and light.

The Godhead, the truest form of what we know as wholeness, is on the seventh level which is the pure energy of God, the knowing and loving being that is all things to all living sparks, primarily love, light, and energy. This seventh level represents the masculine energy of God because it is the power of knowing, great wisdom and knowledge, which is true power. The seventh level is a collective consciousness that represents the whole of God, the spark which gives all life. We are all sparks of God.

Man tries to put everything into a category or box. He feels that if he can label it or give it a name, he can not only identify better, but also not be fearful of what he doesn't understand. We would even like to think of the heavens as a hierarchy to relate better to the order and workings of God's world. Everything is equal in God's eyes, from the Earth, astral planes, other stars and planets, and human souls, to the Angel kingdom. There is only equal opportunity with God. No one is considered better or loved more. We are all unique and evolve differently. God's unconditional understanding of each of us is incomprehensible. The different levels of heaven are not about one level being better or superior, just different and closer to joining the Godhead, which is perfection. We choose with our own free will, in our own way and time, to come closer to the love of God, as an evolutionary process. There is no such thing as judgment or segregation with God. All of God's creations from the angel kingdom to the animal kingdom and humans are considered to be a part of the whole collective consciousness that is loved the same. We are treated with unconditional love regardless of how evolved we are or what level we are at.

Angels Seen on 911

R.C. Webb relayed this story of Angels at work on September 11th, 2001 in New York City.

Staying in the loft of my dear friends on LaFayette Street in Manhattan, I was psyched up for a job interview, and the two espressos gave me a New York buzz on the morning of September 11th. The floor rumbled like the beginning of an earthquake. I thought it was the subway telling me to get my butt out to the Bronx! Gathering up my presentation, I headed for the elevator. The day was beautiful, clear, and crisp. I was immediately struck by the whine of multiple sirens in varying decibels. I was entranced by the urban harmonies as I stepped off the curb.

The real experience, the true reason I was here on Lafayette Street, was about to be revealed. I focused on a fire truck pulling out of its station up the street. Slowly at first, fire fighters half dressed were jumping on. Unbeknown to me, these men were some of the first responders, being the closest station to the initial impact at the World Trade Center a few blocks away. I had no clue to what I was witnessing. The tall buildings hid all from my sight.

These heroes looked like real men, tight faced, jaws locked, steel lips, ready for battle and to help those in need. I wanted to stand at attention and salute them out of sheer admiration. I was seeing them in their finest hour. The fact that they would all be dead, along with 300 more of their comrades, within the next half hour was unfathomable at this time.

As I studied them, I witnessed the presence of their Angels, in the form of shrouds like milky shadows hanging on each man that I could see. The closest man in the cab almost had his entire left shoulder and head hung out of the window looking back at his comrades that were dangling off the side of the truck. Does he see what I see? So, when the firefighter turned and looked at me, his was not a mystified gaze. It was specific to me. Around his neck were the loving arms of his angel.

Beside him, the driver was concentrating on the street while yelling into a microphone in astonishment. I believe that it was at this moment that he knew what was to come. He looked over at his partner in terror. On the back, a young fire fighter finally got his gear on with the loving help of his spirit helper. The truck had passed me now. I remember being stupefied and drained. It took me a few minutes to refocus, and when I did, I was flabbergasted! Angels at work, I mused.

Everyone was running around now like rats for cheese. The second plane was about to hit. Still unaware, I was amused at how crazy I thought all these New Yorkers were being in such a hurry to get to their jobs, studios, and hot dog stands. As I stepped into the subway from where most of these people were running, the second plane hit as the ground again shook violently. Outside on the street, pandemonium had broken out.

A day later, Lafayette Street was deserted. I had been back and forth to the airport three times trying to get a flight out. Each day, I made my way back to the loft, through the barricades, past the fire station, past the mountains of flowers and cards and photos of the men I last saw. I was struck by the beauty in the faces of the men I saw in those pictures and the sheer courage of those left lovingly behind to bridge the gap between anonymity and sainthood.

On September eleventh, I saw their Angels with them. The Heavenly beings were there to comfort them, staying with them as they courageously went to brave the fires. And then carried the heroic souls to the other side.

*Let us be silent
that we may hear
the whisper of God.*

– Ralph Waldo Emerson

4

TIME – AN ILLUSION

*W*hat is time? It is an illusion! It is a perception. It is an indicator that was created for us living in the third dimension or as some people call the matrix. Time is to keep us preoccupied. It is a measure given to gauge the transition from dawn to dusk, from year to year, and from millennia to millennia. We earthlings have always lived our lives by the clock, so to speak. Before the clock, we gauged time by the movement of the stars

We think of time as a horizontal line. At one end is the beginning where we imagine that dinosaurs roamed the Earth. Today we view ourselves somewhere in the middle. And at the other end of the timeline is the future where generations to come will exist. But this concept is similar to the way we once viewed the Earth. It was not that long ago that scientists thought our world was flat. The idea made perfect sense because when we looked off into the horizon, we assumed that we were seeing the end of the Earth. Man believed that he could see where the Earth ended. When it was proven that the Earth was round, we changed our perception. Quantum science now believes that "time" has no beginning and it has no end. Because space consists of three dimensions, and time is one dimensional, space-time must be a four dimensional entity. So, physicists now routinely consider our world to be embedded in this four-dimensional space-time continuum.

My Guides have shared with me that time is circular, never ending. Time is the fourth dimension; it exists outside of the third dimension of space. It is flexible and can expand or contract. The past, present and future are all one when viewed outside of the third dimension. In the spirit world and the heavens, time does not exist the way that we humans experience it. Here on Earth it is a belief system that has been mandatory in our programming. But it is also programming that we can overcome. For me, I constantly move forward and backward in time. During private readings, even though my physical body is sitting at my desk, my soul travels to retrieve information from the spirit world sometimes into the past where I view the event as it is happening in that moment. I will also shift my conscious mind and move into the possible future. When I raise my vibration to channel, I lose all sense of time. My assistant constantly reminds me of the current time. Hours fly by when my soul feels as if it were only minutes. When I do spiritual work during the dreamtime, again there is neither time nor distance to travel when I am in my lighter body. We travel at the speed of thought.

There are moments in everyone's life when we can experience the effects of time being flexible. During a near death experience, you will find yourself out-of-body. It has been documented, and I can personally attest to this from my own first-hand experience. People have reported that time did not exist. It was not a factor; they were no longer limited to three-dimensional limitations such as aging, death, pain, sickness or any other physical confines that we experience in the shell, or body. The events that were encountered and all of the information that they were exposed to made them feel as if they had spent hours in the spirit world. But in Earth-time, it was only fleeting minutes. How could they grasp enough information and knowledge to write a book in such a short period of time? Because they were in a dimension that exists outside of time.

During the dreamtime, while you are sleeping, the soul leaves the body and journeys to different dimensions where time is non-existent. As you meditate in the highest state of consciousness, Earth-time will stretch or condense. Truly enlightened masters have always been able to transcend time and space because time and space is merely an Earthly illusion.

Has anyone noticed that we are coming away from time? In the literal sense as well as spiritually speaking, time seems to be slipping by the way side. We think it is because we are getting older or our children are growing so quickly. We think this about the holidays "How could it be time to get ready for Christmas again?"

But what you don't understand is that time is speeding up. We are truly losing time. One reason for this experience is due to the rotation of the Earth. It is actually slowing down. The signs are now visible of the planet's rotation slowing down. Our spinning more slowly is a scientific fact that is happening right now. You would reason that the slower spinning of the Earth would make time go more slowly. But actually, it is the reverse. I had a scientist from NASA who responded because he was intrigued by my questions. I asked if time was only an Earthly illusion and about the information that I had received from my Spirit Guides about time speeding up. So, he addressed the question and my theory. He wrote back and explained that yes, time is speeding up. As Earth's rotation slows, the magnetic poles are shifting, and the tectonic plates are moving. And the buildup of carbon dioxide in our atmosphere was recently reported as another factor in slowing of the Earth's rotation. The Earth is warming, and this is causing a great deal of natural catastrophic events. Most of the weather-related phenomena have been labeled El Nino. Lately, every odd weather occurrence has been blamed on El Nino. The real cause is Earth changes.

The second reason for this great and special event happening to our world right now is the spiritual cleansing that is taking place systematically. I refer to this time as the ascension, a major shift that is occurring for the first time in the Earth's history. This is an era for mankind and the planet to shift at the same time to a lighter state of consciousness. Mankind is being given a chance to shift to the Christ consciousness at the same time as the planet shifts. That is why we are living in such a special time. Whether people want to accept it or not, these changes are taking place, not only geographically speaking with our Earth, but also within our world religions and societal systems. Everything will change as humanity's collective consciousness rises.

You see we must change, Earth as it is now is about as primitive as you can get. Humanity has fallen into a state of amnesia. With all of our modern-day technology, we as a group are mostly selfish. We were more sympathetic to man's plight one hundred years ago than we are today. Inventions and medical advances have skyrocketed as our capacity to help our neighbor has plummeted. How can we look at ourselves in the mirror? We pay sports and pop stars billions of dollars for entertaining us while children are starving. We kill each other in Holy wars while priests molest our youth.

The vibration of our planet is at a primitive level. It is very low compared to the vibration of the Spirit World or even other stars or planets. It is time for Earthlings to get with the program. We need to elevate our spiritual ideals to become a highly developed civilization.

God has many other groups of children in addition to the human species, whose frequency is so much higher, and yes, more advanced in technology, but, most importantly, spiritually accomplished. They recognize that when working together as a group they are more powerful. Imagine an entire society whose goal is to make all decisions based on what is the highest and best interest for an entire planet. They treat each other as brothers and sisters, always coming from love in their actions, words and deeds.

There are other spaces that operate outside of "time". Heaven has seven levels in which they only have knowledge of eternity, void of a beginning and an end. Then we have the astral planes. Sometimes referred to as "the net" or "the matrix." The astral planes are in between Earth and Heaven where ghosts reside and where human souls travel to during their sleep time while in their lighter bodies. Shamans have reported traveling through a corridor passing beings of every type, some human-like, some Star Trek like. This corridor is a passageway into other dimensions. Souls travel to and fro throughout our Universe. Think of "time" as an onion that has many layers and is perceived in different ways depending on the layer or level of consciousness. There are also many dimensions that inhabit the same space. It is a layered effect of actual places or realities that exist within the identical area.

What we are experiencing here on earth at this time will only strengthen. Each day will seem to merge into the next and so on until you are no longer in the third dimension or even fourth. As this process happens for some of us, we will shift our consciousness enough that we will be able to cross over into a different space and place and finalize the ascension process.

I believe that there will soon be what I call the new planet. Mother Earth is birthing a lighter version of herself. This has been referred to by many cultures by different names. The Native Americans refer to it as the phoenix rising. Christians look to the book of Revelations and call this time Armageddon. It has also been described as the New Age. Every group has a variation of the concept and has a label for it: the ascension, the party, the graduation and the cleansing. If you pay attention to the signs, you are going to see that our world is in the midst of drastic change. Yes, we are going through an evolution. As a group, the planet and the people, we obviously have gone through many stages of evolution in our history. But this time there is more happening than a physical or geographical upheaval. There is the whole spiritual aspect of change. We had a similar shift once before in our Earth's history during the last days of Atlantis and Lemuria

When a planet's survival is in jeopardy, our creator is involved, and we as little co-creators are creating a new reality. We are moving out of the third and fourth dimension and going into the next. As souls, we always remain true to who we really are. Deep in our sub-conscious, we know that this transition is the natural law of God's Universe. There is balance, and once we have moved too far away from the perfect balance of love, then there is a cleansing of the negativity that takes place. There is beauty in the destruction of all things that no longer serve us, and joy will be found once again, as we live life by the law of unconditional love.

I foresee an era where there is no time, as we have known it. Some souls are actually coming into it now. They have shifted their perception and raised their vibration to a state of enlightenment, meaning a heightened state knowing and living a life of unconditional love. Each of us has the opportunity to come into this realization ourselves; everything we do, say, and think affects the future. We are co-authors of creation and can consciously choose perfection, to move away from Earth time and its restrictions. We can experience life on Earth like we do in our lighter bodies. What is twenty years in Earth time, in the Spirit World is just a blink of the eye or vise versa. This is the future that we are coming into.

As we attain enlightenment, we will find ourselves in our lighter body without any physical or mental limitations. This is something that is happening right now with the earth changes that were coming out of time.

I addressed the environmental changes, which

are taking place in my first book. Major changes are upon us, not only the physical changes, but also the changes in our collective consciousness, communities, government, school systems, and financial structures. The way we approach business and trade is also changing. This shift is for the higher good of all.

*Truth does not become more true
by virtue of the fact that
the entire world agrees with it,
nor less so even if the whole world
disagrees with it.*

*The TORAH
- Moreh Nevochim 2:15*

CHAPTER

5

THE CHILDREN OF THE MILLENNIUM

In today's society, we have a new breed of children. They have been appearing sporadically for more than fifteen years, but now they are being born much more frequently. The children that are coming into this world are very advanced in many ways that we have not seen before this time in our history. These children that I speak of have been given a special name from spirit, which is the Blue Ray Children. Other names by which they are referred to are the Indigo Children or the Rainbow children. These souls display amazing talents as well as being very spiritually gifted. They possess old souls in young bodies.

These children are very intelligent and energetic. Working with both sides of the brain, they can be analytical and artistic. They happen to use a larger portion of their brain than the average adult who only uses eight percent of the brain. They are well-balanced individuals that utilize the positive attributes of both their masculine and feminine sides.

For the most part, humans are born with either masculine or feminine genitalia although there is a small percentage of intrasexed babies that are born. But all humans have both feminine and masculine qualities regardless of physical gender. For example, there are those men who are only in touch with the aspects of their male energy: the macho ego, aggressiveness, analytical, and the hunter instinct. They are very two-dimensional whereas men who are well rounded have integrated their feminine side into their personality. They are wiling to show their emotions, tend to be more creative, spiritually open and have a balanced personality.

The Blue Ray Children are well balanced, and they are being born into this world to save mankind. They represent the next evolution of spiritually enlightened beings. Even their DNA strands are evolving because they are vibrating at a much higher level. They are true instruments of God, remembering where it is that they came from, and they remain connected to the heavens and the Godhead. They also incarnate remembering their mission and purpose, fully awake, unlike most humans. These children know why they are here and what they need to do not only for themselves, but for the world. Blue Ray children are very special because they are connected to their God-part-self for their entire life. They can be very psychic, knowing what you are thinking or the solutions to your problems. They remember heaven, God, and live their life by the "Golden Rule," which is to love unconditionally, and they fully understand karma and the consequences of it. The blue ray children will be our saviors because they are in an awakened state while existing in flesh. They will be our world leaders, but more important than that, they will assist humanity and serve in any way they can to help us come to terms with the fact that we have to change and come into the universal consciousness of love.

Unfortunately, because these children are misunderstood by most of society, they are having a very difficult time on this plane. Actually, it is the adults that are having a difficult time with these children because they don't know how to deal with them. These children have an immense amount of energy, and their IQ's are off the charts compared to other children of their age group. These children are gifted in so many areas as well as being brilliant, and some have the ability to heal people with just their minds. Advanced psychic and spiritual gifts will develop. As these children grow, many will start by telling you of their "Spirit" friends or conversations with departed loved ones.

Common sense would tell us that it is not often that you find a child that is brilliant intellectually and is also spiritually awake. Because these Blue Ray children are such a mystery to most and misunderstood, they are usually misjudged. I'll even go as far to say our society wants to put them in a category, but they can't find one that is appropriate. Humans have a need to label or categorize everything. This is the one reason why we have so much segregation and judgment taking place in our society.

It starts for these children at home. The blue ray children need to be understood. But when a child is different from the norm, some parents don't know what to do, so consequently they go about trying to fix something that is not broken. Often times these children will demonstrate the ability to comprehend more than their own parents or the adults around them. They are miniature sages. They refuse to be programmed, desensitized or to buy into the illusion and will rightfully rebel. So they are very open. If you have ever noticed, they are shamelessly honest. They make no excuses for their feelings and for what they say. These children are beautiful souls!

The home environment is vital to their development because their energy levels are high. Their diet should be regulated. Refined sugar, processed foods and dairy products are bad for their bodies, which in turn affect the mind and astral bodies. Dairy is especially bad causing allergic reactions and respiratory problems. Dairy cows are regularly pumped full of estrogen, growth hormones and antibiotics which are carried into the milk. I advise primarily natural foods for their diet. Many of these children reject meat or eat very little of it. The children should also only drink spring water instead of tap or distilled and take some type of vitamin, minerals, and food supplements. No one receives all the required nutrients from our foods today.

At home, these blue ray children need constant attention and are considered by many parents to be high-maintenance emotionally and time consuming. But I assure you they are well worth it. They need structured activities whether it is sports, the arts, a positive hobby or a civic organization that promotes humanitarian acts. This will encourage them to focus their energy on positive outcomes and will give them a great feeling of satisfaction and accomplishment. This is the beginning stage of building and molding character traits that they will use throughout their lifetime. Parents need to be positive role models for their children and know that they are influencing their children in every action they do. In households of two working parents who are trying to raise a family, it's very important that they do not allow the TV, which has so much violence, or video games to play as role models or a babysitting service for these children. We as parents have to realize that everything begins in the home environment for our children's foundation.

One of the biggest challenges is choosing the proper school surroundings. I believe that the wrong school setting can be detrimental to a child's well being. Blue Ray children cannot attend public school. It does not work for them. Most public schools are very over crowded, and individuality is not encouraged. The methods of teaching that require a large amount of memorization of facts, figures and assign mounds of busy work where the child is expected to sit for hours on end does not produce a learning environment for these children. They need constant mental stimulation as well as hands on learning experiences. One of the most common complaints from the blue ray children that I have seen is that they are bored, not challenged enough.

Boredom leads to mischief and a lack of focus.

From a public schools teacher's point of view, these children seem to lack focus, and they are unable to keep the children's attention for long periods of time. The current solution is to diagnose our children as ADD or ADHD "attention deficit disorder." Once this takes place the child is not only labeled as "sick or mentally challenged," but they are put on medications that are mood altering stimulants, which have a numbing effect that supposedly helps the child to focus. These drugs are in the same classification as cocaine. They are highly addictive substances. In some circles, these drugs are often referred to as "Kiddie Cocaine." The side effects are horrible, for their mind, body, and spirit. These drugs numb our children, and after a time the dosage must be increased. It affects their liver, kidneys and they become like walking robots. We are numbing the next generation. Is that the solution for boredom?

What I have noticed while working with these blue ray children is that the school system is quick to label boys ADD. Boys that are coming into puberty seem the most vulnerable because of their hormones. Their emotions run high, they are bored, and since they are misunderstood, they feel like outcasts. So, the ADD diagnosis with drug therapy looks like the answer for a troubled boy with lack of focus on schoolwork. But unfortunately, these drugs do not help with children's emotional issues or their energy levels. The drugs just suppress the problems. What happens when anger is suppressed long term? As years pass the children are like ticking time bombs that could go off at any time. For example, the statistics have shown that all of the American school shootings that we have recently witnessed have been carried out by boys in puberty, and all of them were on some form of ADD medication. Drugging our entire generation of children is not the solution. These medications may temporarily numb their feelings and emotions and act as a band-aid, but the medications are not getting to the root of the problem.

The ADD diagnosis has also been used incorrectly, lumping many children into one large group. In actuality, these supposed ADD children have different reasons for their short attention spans. Some children truly are hyper active, some children are emotionally unstable, some children are chemically unbalanced, some are intelligent and advanced, some have no interest in school, and some are blue ray children who are spiritually advanced. The long-term use of stimulants is not the answer for most of these cases.

Parents need to educate themselves about this diagnosis and the other options that are available. "Spirit" had given me this information a few years ago, but to back up their claims I have included the following research for your consideration:

What has the US Drug Enforcement Agency - DEA said about Methylphenidate (MPH), most commonly known as Ritalin:

- The U.S. manufactures and consumes 5-times more MPH than the rest of the world combined.

- The MPH production quota has increased almost 6-fold since 1990.

- Every indicator available, including scientific abuse liability studies, actual abuse, paucity of scientific studies on possible adverse effects associated with long-term use of stimulants, divergent prescribing practices of U.S. physicians, and lack of concurrent medical treatment and follow-up, urge greater caution and more restrictive use of MPH.

Dr. Breggin who graduated from Harvard with honors, is a psychiatrist, and a leading critic of psychopharmaceutical practices has said: "Children are being exposed to a 'prescription epidemic' of dangerous, addictive stimulant drugs such as Ritalin and Adderall, Ritalin does not correct biochemical imbalances-it causes them." Dr. Breggin continues to say "that there is some evidence that it can cause permanent damage to the child's brain and its function. Pediatricians, parents, and teachers are not aware of these hazards because a large body of research demonstrating the ill effects of this drug has been ignored and suppressed in order to encourage the sale of the drug," Dr. Breggin states that the damaging effects of the drug can include:

* Decreased blood flow to the brain. It is associated with impaired thinking ability and memory loss just as the effects have recently shown to be caused by cocaine use.

* Disruption of growth hormone, leading to suppression of growth in the body and brain of the child

* Permanent neurological tics, including Tourette's Syndrome

* Addiction and abuse, including withdrawal reactions on a daily basis

* Psychosis (mania), depression, insomnia, agitation, and social withdrawal

* Possible shrinkage (atrophy) or other permanent physical abnormalities in the brain

* Worsening of the very symptoms the drug is supposed to improve including hyperactivity and inattention

* Decreased ability to learn

Dr. Breggin goes on to say, "Ritalin and other stimulants are currently prescribed to several million U.S. children in the hope of improving their supposed hyperactivity, inattention, and impulsivity." He presents evidence that these drugs "work" by producing robotic or zombie-like behavior in children. This enforced docility and obedience can produce a few weeks of subdued behavior but has no positive effect on academic achievement and no positive long-term effects at all. Contrary to claims by drug advocates, giving Ritalin to a child does not help to prevent future problems such as school failure or delinquency," according to Dr. Breggin

Many times, it is the teacher who suggests to the parents that his or her child needs to see a doctor because the teacher believes that the child is showing symptoms of ADD. The parents take the word of the teacher without investigating the facts and sets the child up to become a victim to this very common trend of sedation. It is a widespread domino effect that is rampant. The teacher suggests ADD to the parent, a parent seeks a doctor, the doctor prescribes the drug, and the drug companies get rich. The drug company that produces this drug even financially assists CHADD, the largest ADD support group in America.

Thousands of parents turn to CHADD for information on ADD and its treatments that include behavior modification, counseling, and medication. Until recently, it was never disclosed to parents that the drug manufacture supplied money and information to the support group. Talk about a conflict of interest! The only one losing is the child.

For more information you can go to a couple of enlightening web sites:

www.RitalinDeath.com and **www.breggin.com**

Many schools also get paid for each child that is diagnosed with this disorder. In addition, the number of diagnosis is reflected in the overall rating system for the school. Each school is rated, and more students that are placed in this category it helps to give the school a monetary advantage. Who is benefiting here? The pharmaceutical companies, the doctors and the schools are benefiting.

From my experience in working with these types of cases, the children do much better in progressive private schools or home schooling. I highly recommend the Montessori schools because they are a hands-on science based school system. Montessori schools divide children into very small groups and give a lot of personal attention. They also teach the children about personal responsibilities, and teamwork, and time management. They motivate the children to learn by creating interest in the subject at hand.

When children are intrigued, they happily learn what is being taught. Another recommendation is the Waldorf schools which provide much personal attention. They focus on the arts and spirituality. Waldorf does not just endorse individuality by artistic expression but also through creative projects and the imagination.

Another alternative for some parents who cannot afford a private education is home schooling. Many parents are choosing this way of education. Their children are at home, so the parents can oversee the quality of their child's education and safety. Many communities no longer trust the school systems to provide a secure environment. Drugs are rampant, gangs prevail, teachers are complacent, and violence is the norm. So home schooling may be an effective solution for some families. But again, these blue ray children need stimulation, so the parent must be versatile and open to new methods of learning.

The other facet of education that must be considered is the children's foundation of spirituality.

Most parents are most comfortable with the religion of their childhood. But what I have found is that blue ray children do not accept the limitations and nonsensical rules of organized religion. They see the bigger picture and do not understand the concept of the isolation of each religious sect. They were born with the knowledge that we are all God's children, and they are sensitive to the fact that we need to come together. They are already in touch with God and the universal laws that rise above man-made religious rules. This enlightened state is what makes them so special. Parents should take the time to truly see their children for who they are and try to listen to the messages that they are trying to convey.

I am always pleased to see children at my lectures, those enlightened souls with eyes wide, waiting for spiritual nourishment.

One day a strawberry-haired girl had many complex questions for me as she patiently waited for me to sign her book. I told the mother that her daughter was very spiritually gifted. Tina was asking questions that her mother couldn't answer. The mother was at a loss how to relate to her daughter, so she thought private counseling might benefit her child that she dearly loved.

On the day of our session, Brenda informed me

that little Tina often becomes sad, and she desperately wanted to help her daughter who was unusually bright and energetic.

When the 7-year-old daughter sat in front of me, we began to communicate telepathically. Very rarely do I see anyone with this capability. To prove this to the mother, I asked Tina to send me a picture in her mind. With this, I told her I saw a butterfly. Then I asked her to see the picture I sent her. Happily she responded, "It's a beautiful rainbow."

That day I explained to Tina that she is very gifted. She has the ability to see into the hearts of others and to help them with their problems just as I do. This is what she is meant to accomplish. It is her spiritual contract. "You have a very big job ahead of you my dear," I told her. But Tina was not pleased by the news. "I think adults are pathetic," she said. "They worry about things that are not important, and the things that they should worry about they could care less." In the words of a seven year old, Tina was reporting on the pettiness of humanity.

Tina comes to visit me about once a year. I answer her newest list of spiritual questions and nurture her uniqueness. Each human has lessons to teach, no matter what his or her age.

*   *   *   *   *

The other question that I am frequently asked is "Why are so many women having trouble conceiving?" Most people are under the misconception that the physical act of sperm meeting egg is all that is needed to conceive. But I tell you that there is much more that goes into planning an Earthly life. With the council of God, a soul makes a reservation with its mother. When in heaven, the soul looks at different parents. They choose a set of circumstances that would benefit their soul's growth.

Does the soul need to grow up in a poor family so he or she has the opportunity to overcome the obstacles of poverty and become an example for others? Does the soul want to bring a new invention or a medical cure to human kind? Then the soul will choose the environment best suited to make that happen. Will the soul be born to a mother who gives the baby up for adoption to be chosen by a couple who will provide it with unconditional love? There are many lessons that we come to learn, and YES, we do choose our parents, but we soon forget our heavenly choices and mission. Our true goal is to remember who we really are, spirit in human form and complete the mission that we designed while in the heavens.

You must understand that not all women are meant to carry a child. Some women are destined to serve a bigger purpose. Their life is not about themselves. They have come to serve humanity in a bigger way, to be a healer, a counselor, or a teacher. All of God's children are her children.

Have you noticed the multitude of infertility doctors and clinics? In the past, this was not needed on a large scale. We are living in a unique time. Children are not being born in the numbers they once were in the United States and Europe. Souls are no longer so eager to come here. But for those women set on having a child, there are many children in need of adoption into a loving home.

Angels Are Talking

MOTHER NATURE THE EARTH

It is hard for me as an individual to understand the ignorance and disrespect that most people direct to Mother Earth and all her children. Let's start with the basic understanding that all of nature is alive. If it were not for the Earth and Mother Nature's children, we as humans could not survive much less inhabit this world. We as a collective group exhibit not an ounce of gratitude or concern for all of the life that sustains us. We show Mother Earth our true feelings by our actions and sometimes worse by taking no action at all. Worldwide we pollute our soil and water, rape the forests, not only of the trees, but also of all animal life that dwell within.

How has mankind come to think of himself as much wiser and superior to the animals? Actually, it is the animals that are smarter than man. The animal kingdom has an understanding that all life is sacred and connected. One species cannot live without the other because we are all intertwined; everything comes full circle in life.

Some say that animals and nature are primitive, but it is man that is primitive, unchanging, and not learning from our past atrocities.

Even the crocodile, which is prehistoric, cares for its young for at least up to one year. There are many human mothers that cannot or will not even do this.

There should be no question if one race or species is better than another. God loves a dog, a tree, a whale, an Angel and a human equally. All that he has created is loved without conditions or favoritism. We are all equal in God's eyes and each group has its own spiritual evolution.

My Spirit Guides have confirmed that humans do not reincarnate as animals. We have not worked our way up the spiritual ladder of evolution from the elements to animals to humans as some Eastern religions believe. Each group of God's children has its own progression. So, know that you were never a grasshopper.

Don't misunderstand me. The human form has evolved from the time of the Neanderthal. We didn't always look like we do today. Over eons, our bodies adapted to the transformations occurring on Earth, the weather, and the topography. Our physical makeup needed to change to survive.

A question that I am often asked do animals

reincarnate? Yes, animals reincarnate, but they reincarnate as other animals. Or sometimes they become part of Mother Nature's spirit on Earth, or what some refer to as spirit helpers or animal totems. In Europe, they consider them the fairy kingdom, and that's really all one consciousness in the same. These are Mother Earth's children that assist us.

When a domestic animal dies, many times it will stay on the Earth plane and hover close to their home and spend time with its owner. This is very common. I've seen it hundreds of times during my readings, especially when the owner is still grieving. When an animal feels like it is still needed, it will comfort us and stay a while before moving onto heaven. Where do these animals go when they die? There is a level that I refer to as paradise or utopia in the heavens. Imagine a perfect world with snow topped mountains, wild flower meadows, seashell covered beaches, and deep forests, all saturated in the most breath-taking colors while birds sing the song of harmony. This is a level in the heavens that I call paradise, and the only thing that exists there is the bounty of pristine nature and healthy animals that live in peace just like they did in the garden of Eden but more perfect. Eden was created in the reflection of this level of heaven.

Can you imagine a better place to be? A lot of

human souls go to this place in between lives when they take a sabbatical, are in need of spiritual healing or need to rest from the hardships of this Earthly life. Men, especially, will choose to spend time on this level called paradise by themselves where only their Spirit Guide will pop in an out as needed. Paradise is a place of healing solitude that can be accessed and shared with human souls and nature.

While in their Earthly bodies animals can see into the next realm or Spirit World. Have you ever seen your dog or cat watching something that you can't see? Their eyes follow the unseen visitor around the room, at times even going crazy with barking or hissing as its hair stands up on its back. Animals are aware of a presence before we are. Knowing this, a spirit or a ghost will get the attention of the animal to hopefully gain the awareness of the person in the room.

The Shamans of indigenous people have also been able to use animals to shape shift. They actually project a part of their soul and share the space with the animal. Indians favor birds to fly into the skies and view an area from above or a wolf to stealth into a locale and survey what is taking place. Animals are in service not only to the planet but in service to humanity and can be used as a messenger by the Spirit World whether it's a loved one, a spirit or a ghost. Animals are to be honored.

Animal communication is a skill that can be learned. It is a little bit more limiting than telepathic communication with a human or a spirit. Since animals have never conversed in words, they send telepathic pictures and feelings that are much more generic and simplistic. They don't have as much to say. Usually communicating whether they are happy or sad and any problems that they are experiencing. If they have passed on, they give their name but mostly will relay to me in visual-like communication or in a feeling. They show me what they looked like, how they passed over. The same way I communicate with loved ones is the way I communicate with animals, but their consciousness is more limited than humans. Animals are a part of Mother Nature's collective consciousness.

The animal kingdom which includes sea life plays a vital role in our ecosystem as well as our spiritual well being. In my first book, I addressed the fact that each animal represents an energy, lesson or teaching to mankind. Think about this. Without the song of the birds, whales, dolphins and all animals, we would not have the harmony or balance that we need to keep the earth in order. Sound, noise, and music are all vibration, which is energy. Energy never dies. It reaches out to someone or something. One way that the animal kingdom keeps the balance and harmony of Mother Nature is by its sound. If the animal kingdom goes extinct, we have a very big problem on our hands because humans will be next on the endangered species list.

Plants serve as food, medicine, and shelter for both animals and humans. Minerals not only supply nutrients to the soil for wholesome crops and healthy bodies, but they have a spiritual energy that emanates from them that helps to keep the earth in balance. If you doubt the unseen power of minerals, ask how a transistor radio works? With quartz crystal. Your jewel movement watch? The silicon chips in your computer? Science has not yet re-discovered the full potential of minerals and crystals.

Picture our world void of all nature, every continent filled to capacity with concrete housing because of worldwide over population. Farm lands fail to exist. The land is paved for more housing, roads, and shopping centers. Every tree has been cut down and used for paper, building supplies, heating, and furniture. Animals go extinct for they no longer have their natural habitat. The oceans, lakes, and ponds are polluted and over-fished. All sea life has perished. This is where we are headed. Is this man's definition of progress?

As you can see, we are not only betraying our creator and also future generations, but ourselves. Without the bounty of Mother Earth, humanity will cease to exist. We must take responsibility individually and then, in effect, collectively change this world and try to stop the destruction that we have caused to this Earth. Only then can we make a paradise here on this planet.

The fact remains we need the earth and her children as much as they need us. God created a perfectly balanced planet for humans to thrive in. We need healthy land on which to live and grow crops. Trees are vital; they are the richest source of oxygen on the planet. Without trees we could not breathe; without crops for food we could not live. Of course, let's not forget the pure water that animals and humans need to sustain life.

The intricate balance of the eco system is a miracle in itself. Some animals are farmed, and they give up their lives as food to nourish humanity and some simply to clothe us. But what about the rest? Animals are vital to humanity, yet one hundred and thirty-seven species go extinct each day. All life is precious, and yet we take it for granted.

The Mother Earth also gives us natural energy, coal, fire, fuels and gasses. Energy keeps us warm; it gives us the ability to cook and it lights our way. Fires benefit us as it cleans the ground and rejuvenates the places that need purification.

We must do all we can do to make a difference and preserve our Earthly home. In ten years all of our natural resources will be gone if we continue at the same pace of consuming the rain forests, polluting and over-fishing our waters, using fossil fuels and genetically altering our crops. We will have used up all of the resources that Mother Earth has offered to us. We will have squandered them all. Where does that leave mankind?

Through the centuries, we have been given solutions to all of our ecology issues. But man seems to choose the easy way and the greedy way.

In 1900, wireless electricity was discovered by a genius inventor named Tesla. Imagine clean energy that doesn't pollute, electricity that was transmitted through the air similar to a radio signal, transmission that cost very little. Tesla could see a future when eventually the whole world would have free energy.

Why was this never fully developed? The wealthy financiers of the day couldn't make money on something that was free. But they could make billions by polluting the air with their power plants and charging fees for their brand of electricity. And so they did.

The energy and oil conglomerates of today are so powerful that even when some states face sever energy shortages, they still hinder the growth of alternative pollution-free energy, such as battery operated cars, magnet propulsion, solar power, and cold fusion. With their unlimited funds they buy up patents for new inventions. Then they hide them from the world so that they can continue to generate revenue the old way. There have been some scientists experimenting with these new methods who have died under what was said to be mysterious circumstances. This just shows to what lengths the energy and oil conglomerates will go to keep their wealth without any regard for humanity and the best interest of future generations.

For thousands of years humans have been making paper from grass, linen, and hemp. During off seasons there was a shortage of these materials in cold climates. In the 1800's, it was discovered that wood could be used in paper production. So, since then we have been cutting down our forests at an alarming rate. Within the last thirty years paper production growth has increased by fifty percent due to the demands of a literate world and our recent need for disposable containers, packaging, and tissues.

Why were we more intelligent and in tune with nature thousands of years ago? Industrial hemp yields four times as much paper as a forest in equivalent space, its harvest is regular, it uses fewer chemicals during cultivation and processing and the paper's grade is remarkable. Mother Earth has supplied us with many quickly renewable resources to make paper products: bamboo, algae paper, bagasse (waste fiber of sugar cane), corn maize, cotton and hemp.

Why are we as citizens of the world not demanding change? Recycling wood paper products is not enough.

"Why use up the forests which were centuries in the making and the mines which required ages to lay down, if we can get the equivalent of forest and mineral products in the annual growth of the Fields?"

— Henry Ford

We must take responsibility individually and then, in effect, collectively change this world and try to stop the destruction that we have caused to the Earth. Only then can we make a paradise here on this planet. We have created this mess; we must clean it up if we want life to continue.

As I look into our possible future mid century, there is only a wasteland that appears to be left. As I write this, our future looks bleak. But the future is not written in stone. There are many opportunities to seize, possibilities that can change the outcome that are being viewed at this moment. The future changes every day because our moment to moment, day to day decisions are the very things that create our future.

Globally will we use up all the forests, the very source of our oxygen? Will wars in the Middle East escalate to nuclear war? Or will biological warfare be the way to eradicate our perceived enemies through the spreading of deadly diseases? Many natural catastrophic disasters will bombard the lands of every country as Mother Earth cleanses herself. This is the natural order each time there is new age upon us. I see that many souls will leave our planet. Seventy percent of the world's population will be destroyed or will choose to leave.

For the more spiritually advanced souls, there will be opportunities to ascend. The first shift will be between the years 2012 -2014. I have not been given a date for the second shift, for I believe it is because we change our future every day. That is why you are so important. Each person matters more than he or she will ever know while on Earth. Look at Jesus, Buddha, Mother Teresa. Their deeds changed the world.

The fact remains that we need the Earth and her children as much as they need us. God created a perfectly balanced planet for humans to thrive in. It is up to us to keep the Earth in balance for our children's children. Opportunities arise each day for mankind to choose a better path. New technology is discovered, old ideas resurface, and inventions are improved upon all for humanity.

I have been shown through my private readings that there are those who are still striving to bring great discoveries to light for the highest good of all.

A woman flew in from California. She had made two appointments, one for herself and one for her boyfriend Bill, using only their first names. I read for her first, a normal reading with concerns of finances, career, and love life.

When her boyfriend entered the room for his reading, I was astonished to see an eight foot tall warrior Angel following behind him. Dressed in breastplate armor with a sword by his side, the Angel stood quietly behind his charge. To be in the presence of a Warrior Angel is an amazing experience and a little unsettling, especially when this Angel was a part of Arch Angel Michael's legions.

I began as usual with my prayers and added that if this warrior Angel had a message to relay, that I would be honored to be the instrument.

Bill sat quietly and the information began to flow. Spirit told me that he came from "an inventor clan" in heaven and that he was a scientist. He had an important mission similar to that of Thomas Edison. Bill smirked as I told him that he was missing a small key to his newest invention. But I assured him that it would be revealed anytime now. Spirit shared much information with him that day. It was an amazing reading for an amazing man.

The warrior Angel let me know that he was Bill's

protector and that Bill was in physical danger. The Angel confirmed that he was protecting Bill because the time had come to once again give the invention to the world even though the government is not yet ready to allow such scientific advancements to be made public. Soon it would be time for Bill to employ full-time bodyguards.

Portions of the information given to Bill was cryptic. It did not have significance to me. But at the end of our session, Bill finally began to confirm the information that I had given him. It all made perfect sense to him. He was in the midst of re-discovering free energy. Wire free electricity is something the famous inventor Nikola Tesla discovered in the year 1900, but the mega rich investors kept it from further development due to mankind's greed.

As he left that day, I told Bill that his next project would be time travel. A huge smile crossed his face. This was confirmation he said. He had been giving thought to this as his next project.

CHAPTER

7

OUR SOCIETY THE WORLD TODAY

As the song goes, "War, what is it good for? Absolutely nothing." Not one soul benefits from initiating a war. The outcome is death and more grief for humanity. It is a hard lesson that we never seem to learn from. Our world's history shows that we are warmongers. At this very moment, we are at war with terrorism. We are using the "Attack on America" as a veiled excuse for America to go to war and kill hundreds of thousands of innocent people.

Did the Taliban government need to be overthrown? Absolutely. We have come to learn the horrendous story of the Afghani people under fanatic rule of a religious cult. The Taliban denied basic human rights to their own people. Newspapers and documentary video showed us mobs cheering at the public execution of women. Afghan women were not allowed to get an education, go to work or leave their home without a male escort.

So yes, the Afghani people needed our help to

free them from the self-imposed extremist rule. But why is our government dragging out a war in Afghanistan? Surly the United Nations should be able to help the people restore their government to a humane leadership that reaffirms their religious way of life instead of allowing another fanatical government to take over Afghanistan.

Now our government has taken the stance that we must not only eradicate the Taliban, but America will eradicate any government that promotes genocide. Well, that is nice to say, but we as a global society have a horrible track record of ignoring victims of brutal governments. Didn't we look the other way when Hitler first took over Germany and went after the Jews?

A continued war effort only creates more war. It is a domino effect causing other nations to rise to the occasion. Now other countries are evaluating their enemies and looking for a reason to jump into the fight. Various nations hold resentment and hostile attitudes towards America and many of them will join in forces against the USA. We as a group are walking towards World War III, which will lead to the destruction of America and many other nations. This could be the end of civilization, as we know it.

September 11, 2001, was a day in our history that our generation will not forget. It is a reminder to all of us that life is precious and can be taken away at any given moment. That is why it is so important to live in the moment and live life to its fullest. Make each day count as if it were the last because death is not prejudiced.

Through this tragedy, most people have come to the realization that we do, in fact, take for granted our way of life and the people that we love. Watching the twin towers crumble, we saw how the world can change drastically in just a matter of minutes. When we are forced to deal with such a disaster, we then start to realize the value of human life and all that is truly important which is our family, friends, and our relationship with God.

All great tragedies happen for a reason, and humanity has been missing the warning signs, like when Princess Diana and Mother Teresa died within days of each other, two great women who represented immense love for humanity. The world did not see this as a sign of the times, that light workers and humanitarians are leaving this planet. Most people never stop and ask themselves, "Why is this happening?" We as a group of God's children must put a stop to all of the world hate and learn to love one another.

This millennium is a critical point in time for humanity. The population has escalated because all of us wanted to experience the ascension process. The planet and the people are going to struggle through the cleansing of all of the negativity before we can experience the graduation party. This process has already begun; all the evidence is now taking place, for example, when the light workers give up hope on mankind. When they fail to see positive changes, they will choose to leave the planet to return home to heaven. This is the first sign of big trouble. I have witnessed the beginning of this process great messengers of God are giving up. Many are now choosing to leave because they are tired. Having dedicated their lives to be in service of humanity, teaching, and setting an example, many are conceding, feeling that their life's work was all in vain. They are unable to see any positive impact, no real change in human kind and very little hope for a brighter future.

The new millennium will bring more tragedy if we refuse to grow spiritually and love unconditionally as a collective whole. If you have not noticed this in your own life or in other people around you, I would say it is because you are choosing to live in your own little bubble.

Don't buy into the illusions and limitations that have been placed upon us by other people, our government and world religions. Open your eyes and take a good look around you. Pay attention to what people are doing verses what they are saying. Are they living their truth, being what they say they are, setting a good example to all? Watch the world news and get an education. Don't base your opinions on the world from one brief news source. Do some homework and dig deeper. We should all travel to other countries and stay with the people who live there. Then we will get a real education, day by day experiencing what is really taking place around the world.

Be open to diversity and learn from people who are different than you. I assure you, ignorance is not bliss. Wisdom and Knowledge are real power.

Here in America we have had warning after warning: the first attempted bombing of the World Trade Center in 1993, the Oklahoma City bombing of the Federal Building, September 11th Attack on America, and then the Anthrax mailings. What is it going to take in order for people to see the light?

The last "Attack on America" is a harsh lesson for all of humanity. We are to learn from this HATRED, to learn from this tragedy. We must come away from dogmatic religions that teach segregation, fear and judgment. Sometimes it takes something so awful and horrific before people wake up and start making some changes, changes that will heal the world.

We as individuals make a huge difference because together we create a collective consciousness. That is why it is important that we do our best in life, for what we say, what we think, and what we do creates our future. Life should be about love. The love vibration is the strongest power in the universe. We need to live it, come from love in all that we do.

One person can have a massive impact on our world. Look at Hitler and the negative effect he and his followers had on the world. Look at Jesus and the example that he and his followers demonstrated. These are examples of how one person can effect us. The effects are both negative and positive. We are supposed to learn from our mistakes and not repeat them. It will take these types of horrific events globally before people all over the world will as you say, "see the light and come together" in unison so that we have a world left to live in.

Remember this is a part of the cleansing and a shift for the planet and humanity. Of course, we Americans were shocked by September eleventh; it was a day that occurred for a profound reason. This act of monumental terrorism was to serve as a giant wake up call for the world. It was NOT to serve as a call to war. It was a cry for us to recognize that the people of the world are of one race. The 911 events happened to bring the world together and unite us as brothers and sisters.

I have been asked, "Did you know about the twin towers in advance?" As a psychic, I knew something big and awful was coming. I had been in a state of grief for weeks before this tragedy occurred and I had a hard time shaking it! I have known New York would be hit for sometime but did not know how. This is what surprised me and many other gifted "seers."

I can tell you that this attack is part of the Earth's Cleansing that had started prior to this tragedy and will continue. Yes, sadly, more loss of life will follow. I wrote about this in my book *"She Talks with Angels"* in the chapter "Earth Changes."

The spiritual and scientific reason for the Earth changes is that the rotation of the Earth is slowing down, and this is causing the magnetic poles to shift. The ice caps are melting, and the tectonic plates are moving. These things cause a great deal of turbulence on the Earth. The ocean floors are shifting and changing the temperature of the waters. Many natural catastrophic events are taking place around the world: massive flooding, volcanic activity, earthquakes, and un-natural animal behaviors.

Mother Earth is very unpredictable and the animal kingdom is very anxious, what is left of it. One hundred and thirty- seven species of animals become extinct every day. With so many species missing, animals are unable to sing the song of harmony to help keep nature in balance. The vibration of sound has a profound effect on the order of our world. If we lose the whale and dolphin population, this sign will be the precursor to the majority of humanity going extinct also.

During this time of cleansing, we will experience a great number of changes, not only geographic but within our society. Our socio-economic foundation, world governments, world religions, world economics and our belief systems are changing. Humanity needs to come back to God, a God of Love, not a God of segregation and fear-based religions. There is only one race; it is called the human race. We are all God's children, and we are loved equally, contrary to those religions who teach they are God's chosen.

The Native American Indians call this cleansing time the Phoenix Rising. The symbol is of a phoenix bird rising out of a fire. What is the meaning of the symbol? Out of the ashes of our old way of life a new era will be born. You can look at this as a time when our Mother Earth is giving birth. The hurting pain of labor/changes is difficult and agonizing. But what waits us on the other side of the pain and devastation? Beauty and a new way of life, where the world's people join together in harmony...one way, one God!

I have been continuously praying for the victims and their families in New York, Washington, and Pennsylvania! I pray for peace for the entire world. War is not the answer because no one truly wins. Each of us individually should pray, help our fellow man any way we can, and live our lives by God's Universal Laws. We must come from love in all that we say and do. We must come away from fear, judgment, and retaliation. The love in our hearts and our prayers need to go out to all of mankind, not just the people that we know, but to strangers, all of the families worldwide that are affected by man's injustices to his fellow man. I am very sad and hurt by this. My heart goes out to the thousands who have lost loved ones not only to Americans, but to all those involved.

You must realize that the Attack on America is part of the transition that we are in. This is the only way to get us to take a hard look at what is not working in our foundation and make the necessary changes so history does not keep repeating itself. It is a wake-up call to all of us to bring humanity together and to bring us closer to God. Did you notice that most nations around the world stopped to pray and grieve for the lives taken? Everyone felt the loss. Can you remember a time in history that the world came together in this magnitude? Sometimes only through the power of great tragedy can change take place. This was to help us recognize the importance of all life, all races, the plants and animals that we need in order for the human race to survive. We must all change or we will perish. Change takes place one person at a time.

In the days that followed America's tragedy, there were many blessings. Look at the number of people that traveled to New York to work together to sift through the rubble and to help save lives. New Yorkers bonded as a community, breaking down barriers and helping those people in need regardless of race, religion, or economic status. We as a nation understood that it was a time to put aside our petty judgment of our fellow man. Through our tears, this terrible event brought not only our nation together, but also the entire world. Segregation stopped and true humanity was our guiding light. This is the greatest lesson of all. This was an example of how we should conduct ourselves on a daily basis, not only when a national disaster strikes.

But how soon do we forget? Some people have turned their attention toward retaliation and revenge. Our government is now picking a fight with other Middle Eastern countries. America is angry and wants to blame all governments that ignore terrorism. If we continue this behavior, we are no better than the terrorists themselves imposing our will on others through violence. What do we really accomplish if we continue the killing? Are you really willing to send your sons and husbands to fight a war on terrorism? How do you win a war or get through to a group of people that place no value on their own lives, much less anyone else's? The suicide bombers are a result of this extreme belief system. By going to war to kill extremists what will this solve? What message are we sending? I assure you that retaliation and hatred is not the solution. As I look into our future, the outcome looks bleak, and the loss will be more than we will want to bear.

Shortly after the September eleventh tragedy, I was inundated with letters. So many American's became extremely fearful of more immediate attacks.

They worried for their physical safety and that of their loved ones. Our Nation was on high alert.

The fear mentality is not where you want to dwell. As we hear of more bomb scares and attacks that have been prevented, we must all use our time and energy wisely. Pray for world peace and all the families who are in grief due to their loss. Fear only attracts the very thing that you do not want to happen. Like energy attracts like. That is the universal law of nature and God. You make a difference, and if everyone takes a positive attitude and joins together knowing that our thoughts, actions, and words matter, only then can we change the outcome of this event for the better. A change in the collective consciousness will change the outcome. Mass prayers and positive thoughts directed toward an outcome can transmute fear and war into World Peace. Mass prayer is the method that Americans should utilize when we are focusing on the mid-East.

In this war on terrorism, the Muslim extremists have a great advantage. These people want this war, and they are willing to die for their cause. And they are happy to die and kill many people in the name of their God, even sacrificing their children if necessary. These rebels believe that this is a holy and noble war, and it is their duty to cleanse the world of their evil enemies. Many Muslims believe that Americans desecrate their holy land. Extremists look at their suicide as a necessary sacrifice to benefit their people and to uphold their religious beliefs. They feel that they will sit closer to God in heaven because of these deeds.

Our government does not view this war as a religious/holy war but a political war. The United States of America was built on the fundamental belief of religious freedom. In God we trust is our motto. We are not meant to persecute nor judge these religions. We should engage in peaceful ways to resolve worldwide conflict.

Unfortunately, President Bush believes in many institutions, such as war and prisons with strict death penalties. He is the biggest supporter of waging combat against America's "evil" enemies. This war has many facets. It is not only about terrorism, but also secretly it is a route to increase America's economic future. War has always boosted the economy, so now that our conflict with Afghanistan should be winding down, our government is looking for additional opportunities and reasons to wage war using the motive of anti-terrorism as an excuse to prolong war and seek the backing of the American people. The propaganda is subtle. Look at the number of war movies that were being promoted right before 911. The upper echelon of our government knew war was coming. Since September eleventh, we have been inundated by war movies. These are movies to help make the war effort more palatable to the public by showing scenes of heroism and glory, romance and dignity. This is Hollywood's version of war. The fact is that continuing war will only help our children die horrible deaths; there is nothing romantic or glorious about the slaughter of young lives.

What we must come to grips with is that political leaders also use war as a method of population control. As shocking as it may sound, statistics show that by the year 2600, the world population will be standing shoulder to shoulder with no room on the planet for anything else. Our natural resources will be fully consumed in ten years. The world's governments look at us as numbers that need to be controlled. War and disease are two very effective means to lessen the population.

Prior to the presidential elections, I was given information from spirit that if we allowed George W. Bush to become president, he would be the downfall of our country. His policies would revoke most ecological plans to save and protect the wildlife and our environment. It was further explained to me that the nation's economy would go into a recession, and then we would plunge into a depression. I was shown Bush taking us into war after war. I was also shown that there is likelihood that he will be assassinated while in office.

As it is now so evident, Americans' right to vote is more than a privilege; it is a great responsibility. This past election proves how each individual's vote really does matter. It is vital that we vote our conscience. The label of the party is not what is important. An election should be based on "may the best man win." We need to ask ourselves who will make a more positive impact on this nation and the world. Most people choose the leader of their political party or the candidate who is promising the biggest tax break up front. At this time more than ever we need leaders who are in their integrity, humanitarians who are willing to make a difference through being a positive example to the world. America should be the leader in cleaning up the world's environment, saving the rain forests, the oceans and endangered species. We should have successful programs in place to feed the starving and cure diseases. But most of all America should be the example of resolving world conflict through peaceful means. It is up to us as individuals to clean up politics by voting for those without hidden agendas and those who are not being bought off by big businesses.

Have you noticed the shift in our Government? The American people were once able to write their Congressmen and Senators and declare their position on legislation that was going to be put to a vote. But with big business lobbying hard with considerable amounts of money to spend, the individual voter's opinion tends to get lost.

Only when a consumer group gets motivated to go after these mega corporations do opinions start to swing the other way. Look what has happened to the tobacco industry since the consumer group The American Legacy Foundation started "the truth" campaign, the outrageous ads that focus on tobacco industries' actions and deceitful marketing practices. These over the top anti smoking ads target the young people as a strategy for reaching those who are most likely to start smoking. The drop-off in youth smoking rates has proved that when a group bans together for the greater good, it can effect positive change and triumph over big business. Our society is in great need of other groups like this to tackle other societal issues.

As you have noticed, tobacco ads have been taken off American television through legislation passed because of cancer and high mortality rates. This was a positive step for our culture since we are so easily swayed by misleading advertising campaigns. But now tobacco advertisements are being replaced with pharmaceutical ads that are pushing legalized drugs onto our society. We now have a "magic pill" for everything. Have a sniffle take a pill. Have an allergy take a pill. Feeling sad take a pill. Need bigger breasts, take a pill. Sexually unmotivated, just take a pill. If you listen closely to the side effects that are given by a low soothing voice at the end of each commercial, they are enough to scare you into the "Just Say No" movement of years gone by.

Many of the drug advertisements are for anti-depressants; these mood altering and addictive drugs are a strategy to numb us as a society. Most drugs are not a cure; they are only a band-aid to mask the root cause of the issue. Pharmaceutical companies are getting rich, and the masses are becoming drug dependent, all this, as our politicians wage a war on illegal drugs while we are encouraged to pop prescription pills freely.

Americans are turning to drugs both legal and illegal or alcohol to help them cope with their problems. More than a billion dollars is being spent to fight the drug war abroad while 3.5 million addicts at home can't get the treatment they need. The war on prohibited drugs is a front for funneling billions of dollars out of our country. The war on drugs has proven to be unsuccessful. Our politicians speak out of both sides of their mouths, on one hand saying we are trying to clean up the drugs on the street that are easily assessable to our children. Yet in the classroom a very high percentage of children are already on mood altering prescribed drugs given for the false diagnosis of ADD (Attention Deficit Disorder). Why is our society allowing these double standards? Research suggests that these drugs that we are giving our children cause physical and emotional damage. Research is constantly being suppressed by pharmaceutical companies and government control, which the media plays into.

Our society has a tendency to believe what the news professes as absolute truth. All forms of media are edited and controlled, reported truths of what is seen, but what about the other side of the story, or what has been hidden? This is evident if you have ever traveled outside of the USA. European countries are much more open with public information. Our government does not want to create mass hysteria; therefore, they decide what the public needs to know.

Would you like a few examples to prove my point? In December of 2001, there was an asteroid that was a near miss to planet Earth. We were very close to being hit, yet our government did not feel the need to inform the public until after the fact, and when it was acknowledged it was only one line in the evening news. Likewise, in February 2002, there was another confirmation that I know to be true. Carbon dioxide has built up in our atmosphere and is causing the Earth's rotation to slow. This was another one sentence news item bleeped across the bottom of our TV screens. Yet, on the world news we are informed that a pop star was seen with a cigarette although she was a known as an advocate against smoking.

This editing of the daily news is cause enough to question items of importance. We are being spoon-fed half-truths; therefore, we should not believe everything that we hear to be truth. We must take the initiative to uncover the research and know the whole truth. You would be surprised what you can find out when you are looking for it. Knowledge is a powerful thing. Don't be afraid to step out of your comfort zone. This is how we can learn and grow. It enables us to see the world from a different perspective

SPIRITUAL CONTRACTS THE SOULS BLUEPRINT

*J*ust as there is a great deal of planning and work that goes into our leaving this Earth on our physical death date, there is also much more detail and preparation that goes into our next incarnation. We incarnate to learn and grow from the experiences. Our soul will continue to return to earth until our karmic debts are fulfilled and we have evolved to a certain point of enlightenment.

Karma is the law of cause and effect. For every choice there is a consequence. For every action, there is a reaction. Karma is God's justice and design to keep perfect order and balance to all that there is. Karma is a system where everyone is held accountable, God's justice that is above manmade laws where the innocent are sometimes found guilty, and the guilty are sometimes found innocent.

When souls choose to come to this planet as humans, we are guided and counseled by our own Spirit Guide and teachers to help us better understand what we are about to encounter. Each life is decided upon and set up for pitfalls for the soul to overcome. We will choose our lessons and teachings in advance and will be allowed to preview them to see if we are happy with the possible outcomes depending upon the choices that we make in that life. Why are different outcomes available in our planned future? Every choice that we make along life's journey changes the future.

When a soul is ready for its next journey to Earth, it will then view two or three probable lives to choose from. Through a counseling session with our Spirit Guide and the Masters, we will come to an agreement about our soul's growth and the lessons that we need to learn. We are ushered into a viewing space, which looks much like a theater. The Masters then show us different scenarios or possible lives just like a movie playing before us. We see ourselves as an actor role-playing in a lead part with many takes. As we review these options, we will then make a choice with guidance to select the life that best suits the soul's evolution.

Once we choose life, we then set up a blue print to follow as a guide through our Earthy journey. We outline the karma that needs to be fulfilled and make spiritual contracts, which are mutual agreements with other souls. Usually spiritual contracts are made between members of the same soul clan, our group in the spirit world that we love, learn with and that we choose to incarnate with many lives. They are our spirit family much like our biological family here on Earth. Our soul clan is our true family.

On Earth, we will set up signs and signals to jog our subconscious mind to reawaken a memory of a predestined opportunity to meet a soul clan member, like meeting our soul mate. For example, a client of mine met her soul mate through a unique series of events. Sara had befriended a woman that normally would not be in her close circle of friends. She went out of her way to help this woman who was always ungrateful and judgmental. Sara wondered why she was compelled to assist her. A year later Sara dropped by her house and was introduced to the woman's son who she felt a curious attraction to. As the weeks, passed Sara and Mike ran into each other several times in their small community. Finally, she joked that they would have to stop meeting like this. She touched his hand as they talked and immediately chills went up her spine, and there was a feeling of closeness and familiarity. This was a pre-destined sign. Signals can be as subtle as this or monumental.

The blueprint that we draw up also includes

karmic debts that have been accumulated in precious lives. Each soul begins by owing debts from the past. Our soul stores these past deeds, our past conducts, much liked a debit card, keeping a tally of everything that needs to be repaid. Our soul has individual karma, which can range from cruel words hurting someone's feelings to a violent act of prejudice or anger; we must experience every negative action that we have perpetuated against another. We need to feel the experience in order to understand it. This is the way a soul learns through experience. Sometimes a soul hesitates in choosing to incarnate because it knows there is a great risk of accumulating more negative karma in its future life. We already have debts from precious lives to fulfill; this is a major factor that must be weighed before returning. The good news is that once a karmic debt is paid, it becomes a lesson learned and does not have to be re-experienced. ·

In the next lifetime any hurtful judgment that causes a person pain, such as racial prejudice, hate crimes, cruelty to the disabled, or animals, religious persecution, or homophobia will be added to that individual soul's karmic debt. At some future time this soul will volunteer to experience being the victim of that set of circumstances. That soul will experience the same judgment that it inflicted on another.

At the onset of the September 11th crisis, Americans knew that the terrorists were Islamic. Several vigilantes lashed out at the Islamic people by destroying their place of worship and threatening American Muslims with violence. These individual vigilantes were willing to judge an entire religion based on the acts of a few extremists. These vigilantes have now accumulated this karma. Not only will they re-live their actions during their life review. They will also keep reviewing these actions in between lives, looking at them from a new perspective to study their mistakes and understand what to do differently in a future incarnation. They must repay this debt. All debts will eventually be paid, carried over from lifetime to lifetime until these lessons are learned.

Just as we have individual karma, we have group karma as well, karma that effects every soul on Earth. The soul is eternal, and it is energy that changes form. Our thoughts, actions, and words are also energy that go to someone or something because energy never dies. We attract to ourselves what we put out there; like attracts like. If we are negative, we will attract negative experiences. This is partly why history has a tendency to repeat itself. We will repeat a lesson or teaching until it is learned or fulfilled. It takes most souls many lifetimes to overcome the obstacles we set before ourselves. We will keep coming here to Earth over and over again until we get it right. Group karma is different than individual karma because it is something that is completed by those exact souls that made up the group from previous lifetimes. We seek out and become part of a group for the sole reason to complete unfinished business. Sometimes we wait lifetimes before we are able to incarnate with the entire group so that the perfect scenario presents itself to workout this group karma.

The holocaust was a time in our history that many souls suffered as a collective consciousness because their role was to be victims so that the rest of the world would learn from their experiences so that mankind would not allow that type of atrocity to ever, take place again. Humanity sat back for way too long and allowed these people to suffer. It was not just the Jewish people, but also anyone that didn't fit the profile of what Hitler and his organization were weeding out so he could create the "Perfect Race." Hitler felt that they could rightly pass judgment on human life to achieve his idea of perfection.

We obviously haven't learned the lesson. Recently, on a smaller scale, we as a group were allowing the conflict in Kosovo, which was "ethnic cleansings" or genocide. Executions and torture took place in at least seventy towns and villages

Mankind as a group has the tendency to allow ego and superiority to rule, lashing out and killing those that are different. If we continue to act this way and allow history to keep repeating itself, we will not have a race or world to live in. If each person would take responsibility for himself, the consciousness of the group would raise its awareness and become spiritually enlightened.

As a group, we can also see examples of souls repaying group karma in a positive way. September 11th 2001, was a day where many souls gave their lives for the sake of helping others. We lost fire fighters, police and many whose job was in the service of humanity. This collective group set up that day in their blue print before ever arriving on earth to repay a karmic debt as a group. These souls will always be remembered by the rest of the world for their very caring and unselfish acts of their love for humanity. If all of those men had not acted, we would have had many more deaths on that horrible day.

Spiritual contracts

Spiritual contracts are agreements that we set up for ourselves in the spirit world before incarnating. Spiritual contracts are deals that we choose to experience. Our life on Earth is actually a series of agreed upon arrangements that will change throughout the duration of our lifetime from small details to large ones. Our spiritual contracts are all encompassing as we watch scenes of our future life in a theater-like setting with our Spirit Guide and the Masters.

We view all of our possible choices together. First, we choose a gender and a body match for our soul to inhabit. We do not always choose to be the same sex in each life. It depends on what suits the soul's need for growth. Each soul has a theme in every life and a suitable environment that will mature and foster the circumstance to manifests the contractual details.

During a past life reading for a woman who is currently in a same sex relationship, we went back to her last life to uncover the root cause of her current situation. The Masters revealed to me she was a male ruler, a king of a large country who was vain and very cruel to his people. The king abused his power and married only for beauty. During the king's life review, he was made aware of the damage and pain that he inflicted on others. When it was time for the king's spirit to incarnate into the next life, he had three options. The soul chose the most difficult life out of the three to hopefully make up for the life as the tyrant king, to repay the karmic debt by learning the lessons of humility, kindness, and rejection. The woman now has a clear understanding of her current life. She chose to contract herself to be a lesbian, so she would experience rejection on a grand scale. As a nurse, she has learned compassion and humility while in the service of others.

Most people are very surprised to learn that we choose our parents, our home environment, economic status and religious background. Those are the contracted building blocks of the soul's foundation for its earthly life. Regularly, I am asked, "Why would I choose these people for my parents?" Often times we will choose the most difficult road to travel. Remember, this is how each soul learns, through trial and error. Usually, our parents are souls that we have incarnated with many lifetimes. But the roles are not always the same, and the roles are not always positive. In each life, we will change roles; for instance, your mother in this life may have been your brother in your last life. We will continue to incarnate together until we have learned all we can from each other and worked through the karmic debts.

The souls that make up our biological family in life can be part of our soul clan in the spirit world.

We all work together in a group on the other side because we are a unit that is basically at the same level of spiritual consciousness. People have an expression, "Blood is thicker than water." I say, "Spirit is thicker than blood." Humans will often find souls outside of their biological family that they are closer to and feel a greater affinity for. They are a soul mate or a part of our group on the other side.

Adoption is a common contract for many souls; the child experienced rejection and abandonment from his or her birthparents so that he or she learns to be independent and strong.

Beth came to me with questions regarding her two adopted children. She had great concerns about their emotional well being, especially that of her little girl. The children were abandoned as babies and were in need of a home that would accept them both. This suited Beth well because she and her husband had tried to conceive a child for many years and could not. Beth felt incomplete and that she had failed her husband and marriage because she was infertile. The information that was given to me from spirit was that Beth is more than an adopted parent. She is from their soul clan and was meant to be the children's mother in this life. I told Beth that both of the children were exceptionally brilliant. The little girl not only has a high IQ, but also has a very special mission to fulfill. She would one day be a doctor and find and important cure for a deadly disease. Beth and her husband have the financial means to put her through medical school, which is quite costly, and they have more than enough love for both children. With tears in her eyes, Beth stated that her little girl has always said, "When I grow up, I'm going to be a doctor, so I can help people." This adoptive family was in the midst of fulfilling their spiritual contracts with each other. Not only were the abandoned children given a loving home, but also they were given the means to complete their missions and purpose. With Beth as a nurturing parent, she will see that her daughter completes medical school and will encourage her children's spiritual development.

In this way, we all meet up with opportunities to work on our contracts. Contained within our everyday lives are our ordinary deeds and intuitive nature, we work towards completing the goals that we planned in our pre-mortal life. When we choose our parents, our soul will hover and observe our earthly family before the actual birth takes place. Many times, as I am doing public speaking events, I will see a woman with a soul hovering around her. I'm often prompted to relay the message that a soul has made a reservation.

Many people want to know what happens to the soul of miscarriages and abortions. Pro-lifer's are under the misconception that a baby dies when a women aborts a fetus. The truth is a soul never dies. We are eternal. It was only a missed opportunity for that parent and that particular soul to fulfill a spiritual contract. The soul that made a reservation knows ahead of time that it is a possibility that the mother may choose under the circumstances to not have the baby. Abortion is an act of free will that sometimes also affects the unborn soul. The soul will sometimes experience rejection and the sense of loss, which is part of the soul's learning process and the reason it chooses the experience as one of its options to go through.

During the developmental period, when a baby is growing in the mother's womb, the attachment is merely biological, a fetus that can be measured by doctors, something that can be reproduced in a test tube and inserted into a host's womb. That growing specimen only becomes a human being, an addition to mankind when a soul enters the baby's body. Most of the time this happens as the baby draws its first breath at the moment of birth. The soul enters, and a new life with its own free will is created and born into our world.

There are several different reasons a woman will miscarry. The most common occurs when the fetus is not healthy and the soul that is incarnating did not choose to be physically or mentally challenged. The woman's body naturally miscarries the unhealthy fetus so that she can carry the next pregnancy full term and deliver a healthy child. Another reason for a woman to miscarry occurs when a soul that made a reservation will change its mind and backs out of the contract that was agreed upon with God. Reasons for this vary, but usually something drastic happened to change the original blue print or design of the soul's life plan. The parent's choices will sometimes negatively affect the soul's mission or purpose in the child's future that was not a part of the original plan. Also, a woman's medical problems can cause a miscarriage. In any of these circumstances, a soul will be given other opportunities to come into another earthly life.

Cloning

Cloning is the newest technology that man is using to recreate what only God can perfect. Doctors are slowly progressing from invitro-fertilization, sex pre-selection, stem cell research, to the next step of designer babies. We can already choose the sex of our baby and its genetic make-up if we decide, thanks to science. The controversy that exists is between the medical community's advances for the sake of research and experimentation versus the spiritual community's belief that insists that only God can create life. This fear stems from visions of soulless babies being created by man. Let me make it clear that no soul can come into being without approval from God and the Masters. Each soul has to choose life as well as have a divine purpose and spiritual contract. God has the first and last say when it comes to life, regardless of the advancements that man has made in science. Today's stem cell research is doing much to improve the quality of life by utilizing embryos and umbilical tissue. Science will find cures for many life threatening diseases. I believe this is an opportunity for humanity to take advantage of new research that will enhance preventive medicine. Benefits of stem cell research far out weigh the negative.

Our real concern should be the recent establishment of genome patenting. This allows the patent holder in some way to own the individual who is the live carrier of the patented genetic material. The patent holder could then restrict medical treatment and testing if a problem arises in that person's genes. This is an astonishing corruption when a corporation can own the genes located in a human body, and the human no longer has the freedom and the right to have sole proprietorship over his physicality. This is how man's ego can be detrimental to humanity in the alleged name of science.

Death

As in our birth, so it is in death that we choose the circumstances surrounding the event. There are different ways to die, each supplying a lesson or karma that needs completion. We also have more than one death date. If you think about it, almost each of us has experienced a close call in our life already. What we have accomplished in life and how much of our mission we have completed thus far will be the determining factor if we live or die at one of these junctures. Death dates are like crossroads in our life. We have predetermined two or three death dates as possibilities.

I recall when my father missed one of his death dates. He had a near fatal crash with my younger brother in the car. It was a miracle that my brother not only lived, but also came out of the accident with only a concussion. It was months before my father was well enough to even walk; the injury was very extensive internally as well as externally. His spine has never been the same since that day because he broke it badly. Not only did my father get another chance at life, but also my brother was spared. It is a miracle that my brother was unscathed thanks to the intervention of his Guardian Angels and God.

The age old question is "What happens when we die?" "Where does the soul go if anywhere?" Many people believe that life will go on. Others believe that once the physical body dies, that is the end of life. Science has been and is still, at this very moment, trying to prove one way or another if life is continued or not. Science already knows energy never dies, so really it has been proven. Energy can only be transformed from one state to another like water to ice, then changing once again and evaporating. Energy never dies; the human spirit is pure energy. It is eternal.

When a life force dies, whether it is a human body or an animal, the soul vacates and simply moves on to another space and place. Everyday I have personal experiences that prove without a shadow of a doubt that life does indeed continue after death. Personally, I have had a near death experience, but also my out of body traveling has also confirmed the existence of other realms and other life forms. I am blessed with the gifts to be a channel and medium. There have been countless times where souls from the other side have made contact with me to help loved ones that are here in the Earthy realm. Family members of loved ones that have passed over to the other side only want to help their loved ones to deal with the grief and pain that they are suffering. Through the years of many spiritual counseling sessions with people, I have gained great insight to what we will all one day deal with during our own process of death. The knowledge of the journey of the soul into the heavens has given me peace, comfort, and faith knowing that life carries on, and we move into a much better place, one that is perfect. This knowledge helps me in my work but more so in everyday life, to endure and know that this is only one small part that we play in the grand scheme of eternity. There will be many more parts to come. Through the lessons and the teachings, I have gained wisdom and knowledge, which is true power; it is the discernment of it that matters. Over all, the gifts that have been given and gained from the mediumship work, out of body experiences, and the near death journey are all to help me to continue to spread the message that we are energy that energy never dies and that the soul goes on and has many more experiences in the afterlife.

So when the physical body dies, the soul witnesses their own death. We are usually aware of the fact that we are dying which is nothing more than a transition, which for the most part is peaceful. The soul, once out of the body, stops and hovers above the scene, watching with a slight curiosity and even at times detachment. We come to the realization that the body was only a temporary vehicle to house the soul during our short stay on Earth. While in the physical body, we do not realize that in the grand scheme of things our earthly life is a very short voyage. Once we die, we come back to the perception that a lifetime on Earth, whether it is thirty or sixty or even eighty years is nothing in the sense of eternal time, just a blink of the eye. Time does not exist in the heavens.

The past, present and future are all one. It has been reported by many people who have had a near death experience have been greeted by various spiritual masters, such as Buddha, Jesus, Quan Yin, or the Blessed Mother. Not everyone is greeted by the same entity because of their personal belief system and what they are comfortable and familiar with. Therefore, a person from India may see the Hindu God Shiva, or someone from the Islamic Faith may see Mohammed. No matter what deity or religious icon may help to welcome you to the other side, know that there is only one God. All of these highly evolved spirits are God's helpers and assist him in bringing souls to heaven. For most people our beliefs are structured in the beginning, at home by what our parents teach us.

The spiritual foundation that we built on the earthly plane assists us in our transition in death. Therefore, what we believe structures the beginning steps of our heavenly transition. Those people that have no religious affiliations, atheists or agnostics who have not put their faith into any man made religion, are most often greeted by a loved one to help them in their transition.

There are no wrong or right religions. Man has created many different religions around the world. They were created to help man to have a structure to live by to keep order and peace. Religions are supposed to be a way of life, a code for people to live by. Man-made organized religion has produced segregation and judgment although the original intent was to bring men closer to God and to love one another equally. Instead, we have war in the name of religion. It is not for us to judge our fellow man and decide what his fate will be. Each person has a right to choose a faith or way of life that best suits his needs. God honors free will. Why don't we?

Returning Home

When the soul leaves the body at the time of

death, some people will travel through a tunnel and see other spirits inside. The tunnel is usually a gray color or can be a vortex of energy that is very bright with white light emanating through it. Each soul is usually greeted by God's light and by loved ones that have crossed over in the heavens before. We are drawn into and guided to the light of God; it is the brightest light you will ever witness. The sun doesn't even shine as brightly as God's light in the heavens. We all have a home welcoming party to celebrate our return to our true home. The feelings that come over us at that time are over whelming joy and unconditional love.

Once we have been properly greeted and welcomed by our spirit family, then we experience our life review. In a quick flash, we are shown scenes of our life where other people played major roles that affected us in a profound way for the better or worse. The Masters are the beings that reveal our life to us. In a Near Death experience, they will go as far as to show us the difference that one person's presence will make in our life that we haven't even experienced yet. For example, we could be shown our future husband or child. There are reasons that we are sent back to earth to continue our life where we left off, mainly because our mission is not complete. Other times, we are the key instruments to help create a future for another soul that needed us here on earth. These are souls that have to wait many earth years before being able to incarnate at a particular time because they are waiting for one of their soul mates, so they can be together and fulfill their karmic debts to one another or complete a mission that will take both of them to help assist humanity. In our near death review, we are made aware of what we have accomplished and what we still need for our soul's growth, the lessons and teaching that are still awaiting us in our future. This is the main reason that most souls are counseled and told to go back and complete their mission. Many of us that have a close call with death are given a choice to return to earth or stay. You would be surprised to know many souls choose to come back from a near death experience because of loved ones, especially when they have children who are not grown.

As we go through life, we often experience homesickness, a feeling of separateness from God and loneliness. As humans, we try to substitute this emptiness by looking outside of ourselves to fulfill that hole with earthly pleasures such as food, drugs, sex, alcohol or that perfect relationship that will complete us when everything that we need we already have inside ourselves. Our personal relationship with God is the only thing that will truly satisfy that emptiness.

There is a moment for each of us when we return to our true home and state of being. A floodgate of information becomes available to us that was not when we were in our earthly life. Our soul remembers in an instant who we really are, whom we have been in past lives, and what we still have to learn. The method of communicating in the spirit world is unlike our method of communicating on Earth. Humans primarily depend on their vocal cords and a language. But in the heavens, we communicate by telepathic thoughts and clairvoyance. It is an instant knowing, and it is a much more efficient way of conversing between one another or among a group of souls. When a soul makes contact with another soul, they will communicate in various ways. They will send images and pictures as well as the emotions or feelings that they wish to express.

Moment of Death

We are not alone when this process occurs. Our Guardian Angels and Spirit Guides assist us even before the actual physical death happens. They help us to let go of any fear or earthly attachments that we may still have. Fears and attachments can sometimes delay death for those who are clinging to life. When the quality of life ceases to exist for those that are terminally ill, when there is no joy and only pain, many souls choose to exist. At the time of our physical death, the soul is released from the body to experience freedom and soars into the heavens.

Our unseen support team is made up of our heavenly helpers, such as our Guardian Angels, Spirit Guides, and loved ones that have crossed over before us. Not only do they assist us in life, but they assist us in crossing over and make sure that we get to where we are suppose to be.

I knew a great man named Frank who was put into hospice as he drew close to death. He made comments to the staff that his favorite aunt had been visiting. His family relayed to the nurses that his aunt had been dead for a couple of years now. So, as the caregivers will do, they patronized Frank as he lay on his deathbed. He would talk about his aunt that he loved so much; she had been like a mother to him. He announced that his aunt told him that she would come back to see him once more on the following Thursday. Frank was not supposed to last another night, but he held on. Thursday came and he said, "She is here." and then he died.

Members of our unseen support team help to

make the transition easy. They will come to our aid, encourage us, and lovingly guide us home. Especially in the case of a tragic death, suicide, murder, or a swift accident, these events often make for difficult exits because the soul is stunned and confused because the death was so sudden or emotionally painful. People that do not have any belief in God or man-made religion will be shocked to find out there is an after life. In their confusion they need help from their Spirit Guide or Angel so that they do not end up as an Earth-bound or wayward spirit.

Each of us has at least one escort to walk us over to the other side and give us peace and clarity in the process of that which is occurring.

Most souls have no difficulty in remembering their way home once in their true lighter spirit form, especially the older souls. A question that is often asked is, "Will I recognize my family and friends once I'm in heaven?" The answer is "Yes, we identify them immediately." Our loved ones will come to us in a physical form that we recognize. Once we have made our grand entrance and have been welcomed home by all those who celebrate us, then we will move onto receive our life review.

Life Review

Once we enter Heaven we are then escorted to

our life review that is held in front of the Masters, our guides and, of course, the Great Spirit. We are not standing alone as we review the life that we just left behind. There is often times a group gathered in our behalf to help us better understand our review. The group is made up of other enlightened entities, such as additional Spirit Guides, Angels, and depending on the soul and its level of consciousness, such beings as Jesus, the Archangel Michael and the Blessed Mother may be present for this life review. Not all souls need the same council or guidance. We receive what we need which is deemed by the Great Spirit's wisdom.

The life review process is the most difficult part of our transition back home. We must experience all the pain that we inflicted in the life that we just lived on earth. Every moment is captured and recorded within our spirit; it is a tally of every action that ever occurred. Nothing goes unnoticed, such as the times we were alone and all of our interactions in the relationships that we had. We stand before what we might think of as a committee of knowing ones, and then the proceedings begin. In front of what seems to be a large movie screen, where our life is played before us from birth till death, we are seen in our true form. At first it seems as if we are only observing, but it becomes clear that we are reliving our life experiences moment by moment, but this time from a position of unbiased clarity, greater knowledge, and insight. We will not only relive each moment in time from our perception, but also from the perspective of every person that we interacted with. We will feel all the joy that we have brought to others and all the pain that we inflicted with the exact intensity of our intent at the time. As we review our life, we begin to understand completely the bigger picture because we can see things that were not clear to us at the time. We take stock of all of our karma and spiritual contracts, viewing our shortcomings as well as our accomplishments that may have been more than we had planned.

We will see all the missed opportunities and other possible outcomes that we had no idea of because of our limited views. The council will go as far as to even show us our futures that we could have had if we had made different choices or taken different paths in that life. In this process, we will change places and become the other person in our life to feel and see what it was that he or she was truly feeling. This way we not only relive and see what we were feeling at that time in that relationship, but what others were going through. How else would we know what they were feeling and the consequences of our actions? We see the ramifications of our actions as they ripple out and affect others that we have no knowledge of.

We go back to the points of our life that we believed were our worst crises or tragedies because we only know how terrible that it was for us. In our life review we will be shown the effects and the outcomes that our actions had on all the people that were involved in that crisis at that particular time. It is very interesting to see how one person's decision can affect hundreds of other people's lives and that we have a much greater impact on the lives of people around us than we could ever imagine while in our life. We also see the silver lining of each tragic event. There is always good that comes out of crisis.

The life review process is gut wrenching. Most of us have tunnel vision as we go though life, thinking about me, myself, and I, and our loved ones sporadically. But as we stand before the Masters and the Great Spirit, we are humbled by our selfishness. We see the glairing truth of how we lived our life. We are truly our harshest critics. With the help of the Masters, we then summarize our Earthy Journey. We note the lessons that we contracted to learn but did not. We tally up any new karma which we owe and what soul is now indebted to us and which lessons we accomplished. All this information is stored in our eternal record.

I'd like to encourage everyone to look at your life as it is happening. It is not necessary to wait till death. I find it helpful to review each day before I close my eyes at night to sleep. I always ask myself, whom did I come into contact with today? Did I treat everyone with love? Did I go out of my way to let my children know that I value them? Was I fair, just, and loving to everyone, I interacted with?

Like in hindsight on Earth, we tend to see events more clearly from a distance. A woman client of mine lost her husband. They had been together for seven years. At the time of his death, he was the breadwinner, and she had only a part-time retail job. Being very young, they hadn't yet entertained the possibility of investing in life insurance.

Janice felt she had lost everything. Her world crumbled. Her husband whom she loved died unexpectedly, her home was foreclosed on, and their cars were repossessed. She was left with a part-time job and eight hundred dollars.

This is what I call a shaman's death. It is the total destruction of an old way of life, and where the old life was, a brand new life is built upon the remains. Here on Earth this is the way that a human can experience two lives without going through the process of a physical death and rebirth.

Within three years time Janice had rebuilt her life. Because of the death, she threw herself into work, was promoted, and then moved to another city to manage a brand new store. Her income had increased from nine thousand dollars to thirty-five thousand. Because she loved her husband so much, she started to spiritually educate herself on life after death phenomena, and then consequently she had opened herself to more progressive views of spirituality.

As a forty-five year old woman, she now looks back on that part of her life with pride. She understands that she was the architect for her life. She agreed to these difficult lessons before coming to Earth, and she is content with the way she overcame the tragic events. Today she is an independent woman with a spiritual outlook on life. In many ways, her tragedy was also her biggest blessing.

Most people wait until their elderly years or at a crisis point to reflect on their life. But I advise to everyone to reflect on his or her life on a daily basis. If we look at ourselves and our actions without bias, then we have an opportunity to correct any wrongs. If you can truly see yourself impartially as you look back further into this lifetime, you will find periods of life that you may have overachieved the goals that were set up in your spiritual contracts.

Evil Souls

I am often asked, "What happens to evil souls like Hitler and serial killers when they die?" For those dark souls that do go over into the spirit world, they will first experience their life review before going into a special type of healing. These souls who have hurt so many people, will have to experience the pain they inflicted ten fold. This is the first step in letting these souls understand the severity of their actions in life and learn from these experiences. For most souls, just experiencing the pain in their life review would have been enough for them to change and move forward to the next level of consciousness. The dark souls who come to earth again and again, repeating the same mistakes, are obviously choosing not to move on. Some have even come to enjoy the chaos and evil activities available on Earth.

God honors free will, but if these souls are continuously causing horrendous amounts of pain and unspeakable suffering to the innocent, lifetime after lifetime, he will intervene. These souls are the people that we know as innately evil on Earth. Regardless of what therapy they were given, they do not improve.

These evil spirits that have done so much harm to others are not allowed to reincarnate on Earth until their souls are regenerated or reconstructed.

On one of the levels of heaven is a place of healing. This space is divided into different sections. Each soul that needs to heal and rest also requires different types of environments for this to occur. For "Dark Souls" there is a solitary space, a restricted area where this type of specialty transformational healing is done. In this area of heaven, the healers that are advanced will work as caretakers and mothers to the souls that are about to go through this transition.

This process has to be done with great care because the souls that are coming into this place of healing are very fragile. This is a last resort, one last attempt for most of these souls who are to be deconstructed. Their soul's energy is broken up and then reconstructed again. The healer acts as a mother caring for a child. The healer wants to preserve the core of the spirit but also needs to repair the soul by removing the dark aspects. The only way to do this is by stripping away most of their essence and rebuilding it with aspects of unconditional love. There are many facets of love that may need to be added to a soul to make it whole and balanced, such as empathy, generosity, hope, compassion, kindness, devotion, trust, faith, loyalty, charity, affection, humanity, and the list goes on. The healers that dedicate themselves to these souls will stay and work on their patients until the soul is restored to the natural balance of a heavenly soul.

The Masters refer to these healers as the mothers. The mothers will nurture and create a new being out of the core of the old energy. Their spirit has been practically destroyed and then reconstructed with the mother's constant loving energy and light. The soul is in a field of this energy much like a bubble until the time comes when the mother will release her newborn soul. She has acted as a caretaker and helped to develop the spirit back to its fullest potential of balanced energy again. The time that it takes for the transition depends on each soul and how much that it was lacking. This process is one of the last steps or actions that God will take. It is not to be taken lightly or looked upon as a small measure by any means.

This is as close as we come to destroying a life on the other side, and even then, the core of our spirit will remain. Most souls do not choose to experience this type of healing because they feel that they will lose their identity. This is a drastic method of healing. It is a last stop for dark souls. A small fragment of their original soul and personality will still be left after this process is complete. Each soul that undergoes this process receives a fresh start. All of the souls' previous negative experiences from their past incarnations will have been deleted from their original essence. The memories of their deeds have been erased. This is why they usually do not wish to experience this transition, for they feel that it is a regression, and a great deal is lost. It is as if the soul is getting younger instead of older from their experiences. Much like taking ten steps back, no real progress was made. The advantage is that they are not destroyed completely and get a fresh start again with lots of love and support.

The Healing Process

Once our heavenly life review is complete, we will go into a place of healing, a resting place for each soul that has just left its earthly incarnation. It's like taking a very peaceful sabbatical to heal from our earthly wounds that have left marks and long-lasting scars on our spirit. Returning home to heaven is like returning from a battle or war. There is not a specific amount of time that each soul stays in this resting place. It depends on the needs and the desire of each spirit that will determine how long it will rest and take stock of its life review. The level of consciousness of the individual soul will help to determine what action needs to be taken. But the Masters and our Spirit Guide hold conference with our best interest in mind at all times. Only unconditional love is present in the different levels of heaven. We are treated equally regardless of whether we are a young soul or an old soul. As a matter of fact, the young souls are given much more attention and guidance because it is needed, just as a mother looks after her young toddler, making sure the child is safe and that his or her needs are being met.

When they return to heaven, some souls are in such bad shape from the life they just stepped out of that they are considered to be in critical condition and are immediately taken to a place that resembles our hospitals here on earth, much like the Intensive Care Unit. These souls that are in such a critical state of emotional condition will need concentrated amounts of love infused into their soul along with an extended vacation. Different souls will go to different places to rest and heal.

During a past life reading, I relayed the fact that the young woman that was sitting in front of me was once a masculine Viking warrior. I conveyed much information about how this aggressive life was relevant to some lessons in this lifetime. As we moved past the violent death scene and into the life review, I was flooded with sorrow. This strong leader who was entrenched in the beliefs of conquering new lands and killing enemies in the name of the Viking bloodline was viewing his life and experiencing the pain of the hundreds of people that he had murdered. Then he felt the deep pain of the women and children who mourned the loss of their loved ones. The Viking soul fell to his knees weeping because of all the agony that he personally caused. In that very moment, the Viking now realized that his values were misguided and his beliefs were unfounded. Such great sorrow filled his soul. After the life review, this soul chose to be in the solitary healing place of paradise. Even after the healing took place, that soul waited an extraordinary amount of time before incarnating again. This soul took a long time in the Spirit World to learn and evolve spiritually until he was sure that he would not fall into the warrior pattern again. This was the most painful life review that this soul had experienced, and he did not want to repeat it. This soul had learned the lesson while reviewing his life in the spirit world, but now as a young woman in this current lifetime, she was still paying back the karma by experiencing much loss of life of those who play significant roles to her.

I have found through my channeling sessions that a favorite healing place for many souls who have a great love of nature prefer to go to a place that is called "Paradise," "Utopia," or "the Garden of Eden." These are several names used by spirit when referring to the same place. The Earth was made in the reflection of this level of heaven; nature mirrors this to us all as a reminder of our true home. Paradise is a special place and space that I find to be one of the most peaceful and loving places for souls to rest and heal. Many spirits like to take a lengthy stay in this particular space where only nature and all animals coexist in harmony. In solitude, only the soul's Spirit Guide or Angel can come into this realm to check on them from time to time. The Angels and Guides check in to evaluate and to see if there is any thing the soul needs. As the soul rejuvenates, all it needs is to call telepathically to its guide, and the guide shall come immediately. The way the soul calls out to its guide is by thought and even visualization of its presence. Our helpers are so close and connected to us that they can feel us and are attuned to our vibration. They know what we want or need before we even realize our desires. I find that men who cross over with intense masculine energies prefer this place of healing that I refer to as paradise. The spaces and places that healing occurs vary. We have some souls that prefer a certain location to others because it best fits their personality or energy. We have different vibrations and frequencies that each place holds. There are hospitals for very tired and hurt spirits that need tender loving care. There are many souls that want to be isolated and alone. They prefer paradise or just another place where no one will disturb them.

Older souls with a lot of experience on Earth and other planets will go directly to heaven many times with no pit stops and with no escort needed in making the transition from one plane of existence to another. They are usually very excited and eager to return to the spirit world to be with their soul clan that is their spiritual family. The older souls seem to be real pros at returning to heaven in very good shape, and they are able to jump right back into what they were doing, right at the point where they left off in their heavenly development. They will rejoin their soul clan and be with their true family to heal. They enjoy the company and do not wish to be alone. Frequently, the more evolved souls will skip the healing stage altogether and simply return to their group to study and learn. Many of these older souls are even eager to return to earth in another life as quickly as possible.

The entire time that we are in this healing space our Spirit Guides and other very evolved entities are with us at all times. Sometimes they will stay very close by if needed. Other guides will respect our space and keep some extra distance, but they never abandon us.

It is rare but there are some spirits that only wish to be in the company of their Master Spirit Guide to heal. More unusual are souls that return from incarnations and will find their way home with their spirit eyes closed. That's how well they know the journey, and they will waste not one bit of time and go right back into their position of teaching. These souls are always the advanced, older sprits that have the title of teacher. They usually are light workers and have volunteered in their earthly life to teach, heal or do some type of humanitarian service to make a great difference in the world. The last scenario is very similar to the last one I just gave you, except that some of the advanced souls that are light workers on Earth return home to their true state of being which is a Spirit Guide or even a Master Spirit helper. It is not often that they incarnate anymore because they do not need to for their own soul's growth. If and when they do, which is rare, they do it to help to shift the consciousness of humanity to a much higher vibration, a Christ-like consciousness.

Each spark of God is unique; we are all a part of the God consciousness and the great journey we call life. Life continues even when the physical body ceases to exist. We simply move on into a different space and place. But each soul has something in common. Besides the fact that we are all related, we will all continue to go on to follow through certain steps and actions that we are all accountable for in the afterlife.

Life Between Lives

Our true home is the Heavens. Our journeys to Earth are learning expeditions. So, what is it that we do when we are back home in between life times? The soul is eternal and we are not floating on a cloud in white robes singing songs while playing the harp. When souls return home, we are rewarded with the knowledge of all our past lives and experiences. We are given our current status of what level we have worked up to in heaven and future lives that are waiting for us if we want to take those journeys. The knowledge and wisdom is the reward, not to mention the comfort and the love that surrounds us. Heaven is an expansive place of such magnitude that no one knows exactly how big it is. We return to our soul group, which resides in a particular level of Heaven.

There are seven levels of Heaven, and each level is a more enlightened state of consciousness. The higher levels are closer to the ultimate goal of perfection or the Godhead.

Each soul then will decide what it is that it wishes to do individually. The options are endless. We will also have collective projects to work on. With our soul group, we will use the time in spirit to study not only from the life that we just left, but from the Earthly patterns that we keep repeating and don't seem to learn from. We will use our own records to study our karmic debts and spiritual contracts that we will still have to fulfill.

There are many levels of Heaven where we can experience anything that the soul desires. In the lower levels of Heaven to the beginning of Mid-Heaven, there are large communities where souls have constructed their very own homes down to even the specific type of architecture that they are partial to. This level is very steady and focused. The spiritual home and community for many souls, this place took a great deal of their energy to create. Souls created this place by individual and group thoughts and manifestations of their desires. It is a lighter level of reality than that of humans.

They create their surroundings, the community

that they live in, by thought individually in groups. The houses and buildings that have been constructed by these souls are always pristine and beautiful. The detail and the vibrant colors are amazing; nothing has been left out of the blueprints. They even create elaborate gardens and well-manicured yards for their pleasure. There is nothing that you can imagine that hasn't already been thought of and created to fit each soul's design. What is wonderful is that it is perfect and that these places were created through instant manifestation from unconditional love. Everything is wanted and cared for so lovingly. I find this particular level of heaven fascinating and interesting because it reminds me of what a perfect environment we could have here on Earth. This level of heaven is one of the two that closely resembles our earthly life.

This is the most active level of heaven over in the spirit world. We have buildings such as schools where we hold classes for souls to continue to learn. Teachers will instruct on different subjects within small groups in classroom situations. They lecture to larger groups at times. There you will also find libraries and auditoriums where advanced souls will give lectures and seminars. These buildings are for our souls to speak and gather in, sometimes just to give thanks and glory to God. There are buildings that were created to display great works of Heavenly art and a space to be creative in. We come together in places where we can have art classes, gatherings, or shows. We have private homes that are solitary, and we have homes that are in a community. There are small buildings that exist as well as large ones in a community, each serving a different purpose. It is truly a heavenly community that has schools, libraries, art galleries and a place of entertainment. The buildings and their purpose resemble the designs of buildings that we have here on Earth because Earth was built as a reflection of Heaven.

As we move further up in mid level heaven, we see that this space is another level of heaven that is very busy and always moving. It is a very transient state or place of being. Many souls on this level work as helpers doing soul retrieval work. These souls will travel to Earth and help the souls that have just crossed over from their earthly experience and escort them to the light. Sometimes they will have to escort them all the way home to the heavens. They also will help the souls that stay earthbound as ghosts, assisting these souls to go into the light and encouraging them to come home once again. Some souls are stuck on the astral levels, and these heavenly helpers go and retrieve them. These souls that do soul retrieval work are advanced helpers of God and the counsel. Mid-heaven is occupied by spiritually advanced souls that are more focused on helping others. They have come to a place in their spiritual growth that that can chose to increase their knowledge while working as Spirit Guides, mentors, or other positions of spiritual leadership. Their evolution as individuals who incarnate on Earth is no longer necessary, unless they choose to do so. Usually they would only choose to incarnate for a special purpose. Mother Theresa is an example of a soul from mid-heaven who chose to incarnate to bring a message of love and selflessness to mankind.

As we evolve individually, we will chose whether we want to be a teacher, a mentor, a Spirit Guide, or do soul retrieval work. There are many occupations that we may choose to specialize in. We have many choices of occupations; all of our options will be closely examined, especially with the help of God, the Masters, and our Spirit Guides. We are guided and counseled as needed; however, they always let us make the final decision. They support us in whatever we choose to do. We have to learn for ourselves.

Before Choosing The Next Life

All souls are warned and counseled by the Masters and their Spirits Guides not to be too hasty and return too quickly to Earth. The Masters prefer that each soul take the time to rest and reflect on its previous life before jumping back into another. A premature life experience can be disastrous for a soul. If a soul doesn't take time to learn from past mistakes, and it comes in too soon, it takes the risk of creating more negative karma and possibly becoming very dissatisfied and depressed, looking for a way to exit before its actual natural death date, and the death date is an important element of the soul's spiritual contract. There are some souls that jump into life prematurely because they get overly excited. Yet, they readily take the risk of suicide knowing they have been warned. I have seen this with both old souls and young souls. For this reason "free will" is always honored by spirit, even when spirit knows that it is not the best decision for us. The older souls have a great advantage because of all the experiences gleaned through their many incarnations. They are becoming more enlightened because of the vast numbers of Earthy lessons learned.

The younger souls are lacking in spiritual maturity because they have not learned from their personal experiences. The term young soul is not defined by the number of lives that it has lived. It is about how well we are learning and growing without repeating the lessons over and over again. A soul's age has nothing to do with numbers or biological age but how quickly we master our lessons.

After just a few incarnations on Earth, many souls choose never to return to this planet. They prefer to take it a bit slower and learn on the other side where it is much easier because in Heaven duality does not exist, only unconditional love. Humans suffer through the harshness of duality by experiencing much negativity like betrayal, forgiveness, loss, hate, abuse, sorrow, and murder. These are negative experiences in our life on Earth. We live through them, and they mold our character. How we handle adversity defines who we are. Did we take those severe lessons and learn from them? Did we come out stronger, or did we choose the victim role and become constant prey?

In the Heavens, we have all of eternity to learn our lessons and evolve towards enlightenment. There is no hurry, and the souls who find Earth to be too harsh and painful can choose to stay in heaven and evolve, but the process is lengthy and time consuming. There they will study and eventually master the same lessons. They just do not experience them the same way that we do on Earth. These souls will learn through studying the Akashic records. They view many scenarios of the same lesson. So there are two ways that a soul can master spiritual lessons, through experience or though conceptual understanding.

Finally, we get to those very brave and courageous souls that will look and wait patiently for an opportunity to choose to reincarnate again on earth. These souls have come full circle where they started on this journey we call life. They're right back to the very place where it all began. God Bless them, and may they have a safe and wonderful journey in their next life.

You who are reading these words decided to take the difficult route. Bravely, you chose to come to Earth and face the challenges. You came to experience learning on the fast track. The spirit world greatly celebrates your courageousness.

Life is not separate from death.
It only looks that way.

– Blackfoot proverb

THE MASTERS
ACCESSING PAST LIVES

*I*n the years that I have been doing private spiritual counseling sessions, I have learned that one of the most effective ways to heal from our pain, fears, and emotional issues is by accessing our past life records. I have witnessed this and have had the pleasure of many of my clients sharing with me the powerful results that were gained through this technique of healing. The truth is that many people have searched for a way to heal through western medicine, but the solution eludes them. They have tried different types of medications, diverse therapies, and several different doctors to look for the appropriate guidance.

You obviously will have different areas where you need some type of healing. At times, it can become very overwhelming when you have several health issues going on simultaneously. You are forced to seek out different doctors as well as different modalities. You need to educate yourself on all of the information and options that are available, most importantly, what is safe and effective without costing us money that is unnecessary. Not every one has medical insurance to pay the costly expenses. Even when you do, these costs are still very outrageous. Every human being has his or her physical bodies to maintain, emotional states of being to care for and most importantly the spiritual part. Humans have a great responsibility to manage and care for themselves so that they are able to complete their spiritual blueprint and enjoy quality of life.

Psychiatry is a branch of medicine that deals with mental, emotional, or behavioral disorders. This type of western traditional counseling takes a great amount of time, money, and drugs. For the energy and lengthy time this treatment takes, often years, it produces very little if any results for the amount of work that goes into the process.

Western medicine has never been preventative. Its focus has been on curing disease. Surgery should always be the last resort. I'd get at least one second opinion before consenting to any surgical procedure. I am not against western medicine completely. I feel that it has some benefits and can be sufficient at times, but these older modalities will slowly be replaced.

Eastern medicine and spiritual counseling have wonderful benefits. There are so many options to maintain spirit, mind, and body health, such as traditional Chinese medicine, which includes acupuncture, herbal remedies, dietary modification, massage and energy work. I have seen some very good results with Ayurvedic medicine, radical dietary change, nutraceuticals, and mind-body techniques like visualization, hypnotherapy, regression therapy, progression therapy, psychic surgery, prayer, and spiritual counseling.

I have been told by "spirit" that the solution to health issues is combining the two together, bringing balance and oneness. We are in the beginning stages of this happening now. Some hospitals have started to offer "healing touch" after surgery. Others have studied the effects of prayer and visualization. All doctors will one day integrate intuition infused with compassion as part of their diagnostic techniques.

As a medical intuitive, I am able to scan the human body much like x-ray vision. I have the ability to see, feel, and sense whatever physical aliment is present in the body. With empathy, I literally feel what my clients' body is feeling. Many times, I am able to detect the activity in their lighter body as well as their physical body. Through this, I am able to direct them to seek proper medical treatment. There is great satisfaction in this work. When the clients are able to treat an ailment long before they would normally be diagnosed, I feel truly blessed to have made a difference in their lives.

In a recent private session, I was able to use this skill to warn a client of a large benign tumor in her female organs. It was becoming intrusive and was continuing to grow, the risk being that it would soon rupture. I had to tell her on three different occasions to go to her gynecologist and have it looked at and removed. Why she kept resisting is beyond me. I assured her that the surgery would go smoothly; there was nothing to be worried about. Finally, she did go to her doctor, and the surgery was a great success. The doctor told her that she was lucky because if she had waited much longer, she could have died.

In another private session with a mother and child, my attention was drawn to the child who was having a terrible allergic reaction to dairy products that were causing him ear, nose, throat, and upper respiratory difficulty. The mother had taken him to several different doctors, who all gave a different diagnosis, and the child was put on medication that was not working. After taking my advice and simply removing all dairy products from his diet and replacing soy instead, the child recovered fully and is now happy and healthy.

Best of all, he is not taking unnecessary medication. These are just two examples of the benefits of intuitive body scanning that someday all doctors should be able to utilize.

Most western medicine practitioners do not recognize the fact that past life traumas are the source of many physical issues. But the fact remains that each human comes into life with the memory of his or her past lives that are stored in his or her subconscious mind. Everything that we have ever experienced is recorded in these memories, including the ones that are very painful. Past life memories that are still causing us difficulty will leave scars on our spirit even in our current life. I refer to these scars as imprints. They bleed through to us in our current life as reminders of issues or fears that we have yet to overcome. For instance, if a person has endured poverty in many of his past lives, his soul remembers this suffering when his basic needs were not met in previous lives. This soul will usually have a fear of a lack of money and abundance in his current life. Because of this fear, he will usually have difficulty in managing his finances and have a tendency to be frugal. He will also have a fear of not attaining success. Our fears can create the very issues or problems that we don't want.

It is important that each of us acknowledge our fears in order to conquer them. The best way to do this is to go to where the fear originated in the first place. When we go to the root cause, our minds then can understand how to fix the issue. Past life readings or past life regressions are two methods to bring issues to the surface, so they can be looked at closely. The dreamtime will also allow us to receive glimpses into other lifetimes.

Dr. Brian Weiss the author of *Many Lives, Many Masters*, is known for his technique in the field of past life regression hypnotherapy. It is a wonderful therapy if you find a highly skilled practitioner and you as the subject are open to hypnotic suggestion. A doctor will act as a guide assisting you while you are in the altered state due to hypnosis to gather the information from your higher self or subconscious. Unfortunately, you may not get the results or clarity that you are seeking because the hypnotist cannot do the work for you; the hypnotist is just guiding you through this process. Some people cannot be hypnotized and others only to varying degrees. When it is successful, you have to trust the visions and information that is coming from your own memories of those experiences through your spirit. People have a tendency to doubt the information sometimes, thinking that it was their imagination. The intellectual mind will rationalize the experience and act like a filter for the information that is coming through to us from our higher self. This technique can be very effective and helpful to a person who is working with a doctor or counselor that he or she trusts.

A past life reading is done with a medium that can channel the information to you from the Akashic records. The medium is doing the work and gathering as much detail needed for the client. The medium has to have a pure intent and respect the authority of the Masters as well as the privacy of the client's sacred documents. Without the council giving permission, the records could not be accessed successfully. The medium will go into a meditative state and raise her vibration and after being allowed to access, then she will go to the library to look at the Akashic records of that individual.

Not too long ago a very nice client of mine named Barbara came into my office to get a past life reading to help her understand why she was having the challenges in her current life. It was one of the most interesting past life readings I have experienced in years. I start all of my sessions by going into prayer and meditation to retrieve records while in an altered state. All past life information is kept in the Akashic records.

The information is channeled directly from the Masters or council. They must grant me permission to view the past lives that my client needs to review because of the negative karma and spiritual contracts that have flowed over into her current life.

As I was channeling the details and the information to her, I felt as if I were watching a movie, observing quietly while it played before my eyes. The information about her first life that I was given told me that she was an Amazon warrior in a time where women ruled. She was the leader of her tribe and highly respected by her clan. Strikingly beautiful with fiery red hair that was worn wild, she was an Amazon warrior that was very tall with long legs and fair skin. Her appearance was unique, marked by her odd coloring of hair and skin. She was born with the gift of "seeing" and considered to be a mystic and leader to her people. This high-ranking warrior was the closest to her queen and second in command. It was a very physically demanding life that she had no problems in keeping up with. Her strength was amazingly close to that of a man.

An enemy tribe attacked the warriors and her clan. The leader of the opposing tribe snuck up on the red haired warrior and attempted to take her life violently by slitting her throat from behind. She succeeded in doing just that, but Barbara caught her by the arm and managed to throw her off balance, but not enough to stop her enemy from cutting her throat wide open. This was a great victory for the enemy but shame to the leader who lay bleeding to death. Her sister warriors picked up her body and took her to the medicine women to sew her neck wound up. The proud warrior would have been happier to be left to die because she was humiliated, and her tribe lost honor for there was no victory for her clan. This Amazon warrior was a powerful woman with icy blue eyes, full armor, and an exceptional headdress to state her ranking.

Now, she could not come to terms living as a mute within her tribe. She wanted to forfeit her life, but this was not acceptable to her people. She had lost her strength and more importantly her voice. Because her vocal cords were severed, she could no longer lead her people and in despair, isolated herself from her sister warriors. In the end, she took her life, making it look like it was an accident by drowning as her canoe flipped on the surface of the water. In her physical death, she would not allow her spirit to move into the light. She remained earthbound haunting the grounds and people that she loved. As time passed, she witnessed the bloodshed and destruction of her home and family. Eventually, she went into the light and returned to heaven.

In the second lifetime that I viewed, there was another clue to her issues. In this incarnation, Barbara was again female. The era that she was living in was the Wild West, during the time of the cowboys. She was a white woman who was married, living in a small town in Arizona. The majority of the people here treated the Native Americans unjustly. She was constantly sticking up for the Indians and received much ridicule from the community. Although it was not common practice because she was always meddling in Native Issues, eventually a lynch mob hung her for speaking on the behalf of the Native Americans too much.

My client Barbara could relate to the wild west life best and understood why she was having the challenges in her current life. As a public speaker, teacher, and writer, Barbara often is in a position where she has to express herself verbally; her career is dependent upon on her ability to vocalize issues, some of which are controversial. Until this past life reading Barbara couldn't understand why she would have panic attacks. Her throat would feel as if it were closing, and sometimes she would be emotionally overwhelmed. As a result, these symptoms began to hinder her career. In two of her past lives that we viewed, she had issues as a result of throat injury. In the first one, her throat was slashed and she lost her ability to speak. In the second one, she was hung because she spoke her opinions and died as a result. So, in this life she has carried over those scars as soul imprints. Before incarnating in this present life, she choose to come in as a speaker in order to balance out the karma and also to heal these scars. After she had her past life reading and recognized these issues and more importantly from where they stemmed, she was able to let that fear go and move on.

I found the information to be very interesting. Not only did it make sense to her, but it also helped to heal her current fears on this physical and emotional level. The past life reading explained who Barbara was in several lives and how she developed and evolved to who she is today. Past life readings are a way for everyone to look at past issues that carry over into the present.

INTO THE DARKNESS

*P*oltergeists, possessions, ghostly torment, this sort of evil has been labeled as fiction. The fact is that there is much darkness on the Earth plane and astral levels. In the Heavens, we are only subjected to God's unconditional love and light. But on Earth, while we are trapped in human form, we are forced to deal with lower, evil entities, things that really do go bump in the night. There are many famous places around the world that are known to be haunted, and if we look back through history, there are some people that have been documented for being possessed by evil spirits. However, not all spirits or ghosts are evil. What determines if a spirit is good or bad is its actions or behavior towards the living. Ghosts are Earth-bound souls that didn't cross over into the light of heaven at the time of their physical death. The reasons for delaying their moving into the next realm will vary for each soul. Some ghosts choose to stay earthbound because of love. They are still in love with their mate and do not wish to leave them, so they hover close by and wait for their mate's physical death, and then they will cross over hand in hand to heaven. Murder victims and suicides are the most common scenarios for producing wayward ghosts. These deaths which are usually very horrific and tragic cause confusion for many spirits especially because their deaths are so sudden and unnatural. In their confusion and restlessness, they are not ready or willing to pass over into the light. Their spirit is attached to earthly things whether that is drugs, sex, food, or people. These earthly attachments and addictions keep them earth bound, and they cannot leave until they no longer have this need or desire. These souls/ghosts have free will even when they have experienced physical death. They have to want to go to the light and make the journey home to heaven; they cannot be forced to go on. It is common with many murder victims that the souls stay earthbound because they are seeking justice and peace. Many souls that choose to take their own life before their natural death date have to deal with the fact that they broke one of the major laws of God that is not taken upon lightly by Spirit. It is considered a waste of a human body and life. A lot of suicides have to deal with their guilt and their own judgment of what they have done. Their judgment or belief system can hold them between realms as a wayward ghost. Some soul cannot leave the Earth realm until they reach their original death date.

The reasons that we have ghosts are many, one being that if someone in life believed that there was a place such as hell, that soul could choose to stay on earth out of fear of being thrown in such an awful place that religion has depicted. Some souls stay earthbound because they are attached to a physical place such as a home or property. It depends on the personality and attributes that make for a good ghost or a bad ghost.

We have all heard people say, "Wow, he is not acting like his usual self!" or "I can't believe she just did that. It's not like her at all!" Most of the time this is caused from having a really bad day, or our hormones are out of whack, even puberty. But what if it is not any of those things? What if there is no reasonable explanation for your child's seeming one hundred and eighty degree personality change? Surely puberty won't cause your normally well mannered twelve year old to, among other things, chase you with a sharp object or speak to you in a unnatural voice. So, what is wrong? Could it be a possession? The equally important question is how do you get rid of it? You get rid of an entity by finding someone like myself to perform an exorcism. I perform exorcisms primarily on children because the innocent need protection. They can become very violent and aggressive with the strength of ten men. It is much easier to keep a child under restraint than it is a grown man. I have a great love and affinity for children, that is what primarily called me into this special field.

The next section is a conversation that I had with a colleague on the topic.

Q: How is a clearing and blessing different from an exorcism?

A clearing is the removal of a negative energy from a place and blessing it with prayer and a ceremony. That is a much easier task than removing an entity from a person. This is a very exclusive field. Not many people have the knowledge or experience in this area, and if they do, they do not usually have a desire to do this work, regardless of how much money would be paid because of the danger that is involved.

Q: What is an exorcism and why is it needed?

An exorcism is vanquishing an entity that has attached itself to a human. If the entity is a negative wayward spirit and has found a vehicle, you must rid the person of this spirit-hitchhiker that has caught a free ride. The reason for this is that they can do harm to the person who has become their living host; they are now two souls sharing one body. A possession is different than a haunting because in a haunting, the ghost is attached to a house or property and you find yourself living together, sharing the same space with an unwanted guest.

In order to perform a successful exorcism, people assume that you just have to call upon your local priest or rabbi. For those people that do not participate in any man-made religions, there are other ways to go about seeking help in finding someone who can perform an exorcism without a religious title and are still qualified as well as experienced. It is not the title or religion that will guarantee a successful clearing or exorcism; it is primarily the person's faith. Another route for those people that do not choose to go the western way or man-made religion would be to look for a shaman or psychic-medium that does this particular work. Remember, it is not the title or even the ceremony that will determine the outcome, but more importantly, it is the person's intent, goodness, purity of spirit, heart, and an unbending amount of faith and no fear. Then you have likely already won. I work with all of those things, but I am blessed with the assistance of the Archangel Michael as well. He works by my side aiding me in fighting evil and helping to vanquish the spirit or spirits from the person or place. Even if a soul chooses not to go to the light, you can remove it from the person or place. I'm also fortunate to be a psychic-medium, which gives me an upper hand with regards to communicating with the ghost. Communication is a key ingredient as well as the knowledge of the rituals and ceremonies to perform. I'm able to see, hear, and feel the spirit or sprits. My communication skills are very broad and help in this service that I offer to humanity. It is a blessing, and I am thankful for this gift. I am simply the instrument.

Q: Can anyone who is psychic perform an exorcism?

Just because you are a psychic or a medium does not mean that you can do this work. Most people cannot, and of those that are capable, even a smaller percentage choose to work in this area. It can be extremely dangerous; it is very exhausting and takes a great deal of energy. Even the Catholic church has for the most part, lost the ability to vanquish the forces of evil; the knowledge was not passed down to the younger priests. This way has been lost because the older priests had no one with purity of heart to transfer their ceremonial ways to. Many years passed before the church saw a real need like today. Now the demand is great, and the church has been overwhelmed with requests for exorcisms. Presently, I only know of one elderly priest that is still doing this work successfully.

There are two important ingredients to be an exorcist, a tremendous amount of unbending faith and purity of spirit. My being a psychic-medium just happens to enhance these attributes by being able to actually see and hear the spirit.

It is not my favorite type of spiritual work. I have never advertised the fact that I perform exorcisms. And I don't look for it; it's something's that finds me.

Q: Are there people who walk around with several spirits attached to them?

Oh yes, and that is very scary! I have noticed that this is more common with adults that have very addictive personalities. Some people are literally a target for wayward ghosts because they have no faith in God and do nothing to protect themselves. Wayward spirits can be attracted to a person for a specific reason, like having a similar evil personality trait or an addiction that the ghost had in life.

For example, a wayward spirit that was an

alcoholic or a drug addict will look for a host in the physical world with the same obsession. Earth-bound spirits are going to gravitate toward someone that can feed their desire for excessive drinking and heavy drug use. No, the spirit cannot pick up the glass and drink or inject drugs, but it feeds off the person's aura, his essence, his energy, and negatively influence the person to ingest more substances and lash out in violence. These types of people can have multiple entities with them.

Likewise mass murders are often possessed; they welcome the darkness and attract twisted evil entities with their very thoughts. Murderers that reveal that they have no memory of their violent crimes are many times truthful. This is because the Earth-bound spirit was in control of their body and mind. This is called a possession when a spirit has taken over.

Q: What about children? Why do possessions happen to the innocent?

Of the cases that I have worked on with children, there seems to be a pattern. In every case thus far, the possession has been a young boy in puberty diagnosed ADD (Attention Deficit Disorder), bipolar disorder, emotional detachment, or other behavioral problems, who has been medicated with legitimate prescription drugs.

Due to the medication, the children's minds are clouded, and their natural defense mechanism is not working. This makes the children more vulnerable, and they are unable to fight off these entities.

Q: How do you find out about these children?

During a private counseling session with a parent, my Spirit Guides or the child's gives the information to me. Parents are not really educated about the side effects of the ADD or ADHD drugs. The Spirit World has told me that long-term scientific studies of these drugs will show that they do great emotional as well as physical harm to children. They hinder emotional growth by suppressing the child's feelings, and in most cases anger and rage will surface and continue to escalate. The individual child never learns to express himself in a productive fashion. Consequently, drug dosages are regularly increased to keep the child repressed and controllable.

Spiritually speaking, the drugs shut down their natural defense system. When anyone, an adult or child, is numbed with a chemical for a period of time, he or she is open to an invasion from a strong Earth-bound spirit. A wayward soul will attach itself to a human to feed off of the life force if it can.

Q: When you say attached, do you mean the spirit is actually inside the body of the person?

Yes, the spirit can attach itself to the physical body of its host, which then requires a full blown out exorcism. The spirit travels with the person, sharing the body. But there are several other scenarios as well. The entity can also just be in the house to be around its host just waiting for the opportunity to attach itself. Or the ghost may only be attached to the place; it has no regard to the people who reside there. This is the difference between a possession and a haunting.

Q: When an exorcism is performed successfully, where does the spirit go?

That is the thing about free will. When you're dealing with these entities or ghosts, you cannot make a spirit go to the light. Spirits choose where they go, and I have to try to educate the spirit by way of a telepathic clairvoyant language. They need a reason to go into the Heavens. Family and friends awaiting their arrival on the other side will often help by welcoming and escorting them to heaven. A portal or doorway will open to allow them through. Thanks to the family, this makes my job easier.

These entities will do all kinds of things to scare you off; they want to stop you from your mission of clearing them from the place or the person. The fact that I communicate with them, see, feel, hear, and smell them, helps me to coax them into leaving and going onto the heavens. I tell them how great it is and try to describe the experience to them. Again, it is their choice, and they will either choose to go to the light or they won't. There have been a few cases where they were very adamant and persistent and would not go over. When they will not willingly go to the light, I have been able to remove them from the person and the place. I have been able to vanquish them from that very spot, never to return again. Thanks to my unseen support team, I was very fortunate to be able to get rid of the spirit being attached to the child and to the place.

Q: *Why would a wayward spirit pick one child over another? Don't these parents ask "Why my Child?"*

An entity will choose the child that is usually the most vulnerable, the most open to a possession. I find that many times children are not really fully aware of it. A possession is like an intrusion. They can't really explain the things that are happening to them because it has been a gradual progression of the entity's influence over them. There are typical signs of the children being possessed, and there are degrees of how extreme these cases can be. But a lot of them have what I call a full-blown possession. They will have terrible nights, they refuse to sleep in their room alone, they lash out, and make threats of bodily harm to their parents and are violent. Sometimes they even speak out in a strange voice, even cursing at times. Once I heard the voice of a man come out of a small child. It was shocking.

Other children realize that they have someone with them, and they are not really happy about it, but they don't know how to get rid of the spirit. So, it just depends on the child. But what it boils down to is that the negative spirit is attracted to the child's light or energy. That particular child is an easy target, and the spirit can get in.

Q: Do you need the child's cooperation to get rid of the spirit?

Well, it most certainly makes my job easier. When I have the child's cooperation, usually when we have met prior to the exorcism, he or she trusts me; children have wonderful intuition. They know who you really are and what your true intent is. If they feel comfortable and safe, and they know that I'm there to help them eliminate their problem, then it is a less arduous process. But no, I don't have to have the child's cooperation to get the job done.

Q: What do you actually see when the spirit leaves and moves into the heavens?

Well each case is different. Once I was asked to get rid of a ghost in a high-rise apartment building. It was a studio apartment where an elderly man named Eddie had died. The new owner could feel the spirit at times.

As I arrived, I could feel the heavy presence emanating from the small apartment. There was a cold spot in one corner of the room. Ken the owner told me that this was the spot where Eddie had died in his bed. As I stood in the center of the room, the spirit was darting from place to place as if he were trying to hide from me. He knew that I was there to vanquish him. Water started to leak from the bathroom sink. I could hear the loud dripping, so I went to investigate. Eddie was trying to scare me. I moved back into the main area. The kitchen exhaust fan turned on by itself.

As I performed my ceremony, I concentrated on his spirit. He was a lonely man who had turned into a hermit in his old age and his apartment was still his refuge even in death. I was telepathically communicating with him, encouraging him to move into the heavens. But he had no religious belief and no real desire to go anywhere.

My Spirit Guides showed me that in life this man had served in the military during wartime. This was the period in Eddie's life that he had developed deep friendships. This was the key. Now I was able to tell the spirit that his buddies were on the other side waiting for him. This got his attention. As I lovingly spoke of his friends, a vortex opened up. These young men in military uniform were waving to him, motioning for him to come with them. They showed themselves to Eddie just as he would remember them. As he crossed over into the tunnel, his friends were smiling and patting him on the back. It was a happy reunion. Then the vortex closed.

Q: *What is a clearing & blessing?*

A clearing and blessing is a ceremony that I am called upon to perform at a specific location whether it be a commercial or a residential property. People ask me to visit their business or their home simply to spiritually cleanse and bless the locale, to remove any negative energy that continues to reside there. Usually, I find a large amount of negative energy that is a lingering residue from previous tenants. This procedure is relatively simple but necessary. Positive energy in a space makes for positive interactions.

On rare occasions, there is an imprint that needs to be removed. An imprint is the energy of a negative event that has left a mark on time and space. Let's say someone was killed very tragically, a suicide or a murder, and the violence was very horrific. The soul of the person has moved on into the light, but the event itself leaves a scar on time, in our version of time. Then the same violent act will play itself out at the exact time every night, or whenever the event took place. It's like a video or I should say a motion picture, where the tape roles but you only see one event playing itself out over and over again.

At times people confuse an imprint with an actual haunting. But an imprint is redundant. The same exact scene plays over and over until it fades out or is cleared. An imprint is the negative remains from an event. There is actually a drastic difference between an imprint and a haunting/possession.

Q: So an Imprint is different than a ghost?

A haunting occurs when you have an entity with free will roaming the Earth, residing in a place, or attached to a person. By the way, not all ghosts are bad or malcontent. If you are under the misconception that all spirits and ghosts are evil, that's just not true. Just like in every day life, you have good loving people and you have negative hateful people. You have some spirits that are simply just mischievous or bored, some are afraid to go into the light, and others are actually helpers to the living. So again this is just like in life people are very different. They have their unique personalities, and ghosts are the same way. They are just in a lighter body.

An imprint is not a spirit. It is a holographic image. Here in South Florida there is a famous hotel that still carries an imprint from the 1920's. A lady was shot and killed in a lover's triangle. Two men were quarreling over her on a staircase and this hotel has had the imprint of this scene playing itself out every night around midnight. It is like seeing a movie of the murder and a shooting. Every night at midnight, this scene will play itself out until it fades. It was a very violent, very shocking act that has left a scar on that time and place, like when we have a wound and it leaves a scar or a mark. That's why an imprint is sometimes referred to as a scar or a bleed through. Until it dissipates, until it no longer holds that intense energy, only then will it fade out. It will no longer be there like a memory recorded in time on that place. It is like history keeping a record to remind us of what happened and hopefully not to be repeated it again.

Q: So eventually all imprints will fade?

Yes, eventually. Some imprints take longer than others to dissipate because the energy is very strong and intense; as time passes, the scar becomes lighter and lighter until it can no longer be seen.

Q: *Can anyone see them or only certain people attuned to those events?*

Anyone can see them, but I have found that not everyone does see them. Usually, it is those who are a bit more intuitive.

Q: *Are imprints only where the violence is so severe like that of battlegrounds or concentration camps?*

Most certainly, there are many places today that you can go that are actually haunted by spirits from the past. Then there are certain places that simply just have scarring imprints on them all over the world, but especially places where there has been a great amount of violence over and over. Europe is considered old country. There is so much more history there than in the United States. Many more people over the years have lived and died in Europe due to wars, diseases, murders and suicides that have taken place, so there are many more hauntings and imprints.

Q: *Do ghosts seek you out?*

Both ghosts and heavenly spirits will often indirectly nudge their loved ones to seek me out. Not too long ago, a young woman came for a channeling session. There was someone who was on the other side that she wanted to contact. Even before my prayers were completed, there was a male presence in the room.

He was a young, handsome man in a dark uniform with a gun. Either a police officer or armed security guard I said. Immediately the young woman began to cry. "Is this who you wanted to contact," I asked? Yes, I was correct, and she handed me a photograph of her husband David in a police uniform.

I intuitively knew that the wife had many questions surrounding the death of her husband; she had been told it was suicide by gunshot.

I see your husband. He is bound by ropes sitting in a chair in the center of a well-lit room. There are cops standing around him. They are in the midst of an intense discussion. One of David's closest friends walks up and shoots him. Your husband wants you to know that he did not take his own life. There has been a cover up. He is worried that you are in physical danger, and he has been watching over you and your children. He is choosing to remain Earth-bound until you both have some closure about his tragic death. Eventually, he will go into the light when he has peace with the situation.

David went on to tell me that he and his coworkers were involved in illegal activities. He was made the scapegoat in these illicit actions and internal affairs was questioning him. His partners soon considered him the weakest link and feared that the truth would soon be disclosed, so they killed him.

He went on to say that he did not want his wife to pursue avenging his murder. It would only be in vain. There was no evidence due to the extensive cover up, and his partners would not break the code of silence. He wanted her to know the truth, to be safe, and move their family to another state.

Q: Are some ghosts afraid to leave the Earth because they fear judgment and hell?

Yes, many people fear hell. Dogmatic religion has created this whole control mechanism. None of us have led a perfect life. So, at the time of death a soul can choose to stay Earth-bound out of fear. Man-made religions have done a disservice to mankind by fostering a belief in hell.

Q: Are you saying that hell does not exist?

God did not create "the hell" that we have been taught or programmed to believe in by man-made religions. Our Creator did not bring into being a man with a pointy tail that lives in a place filled with brimstone and fire. The way religion presented this concept to the masses was about control, the ultimate way of scaring the hell out of you so you would never question or doubt the religious commandments as they were introduced. This insured that you would do what you were told to. So, that is how this whole space and place was created on the astral levels by the collective consciousness that bought into this belief system.

Now what has happened since religion invented this concept? Human souls have actually manifested these lower astral levels that are hell-like. At the time of physical death, when some souls leave their body and cross over, they are so entrenched in their belief system that in their minds, they think that they are not worthy, that they deserve to go to this place that religion calls hell. So by their own free will they place themselves on a lower astral plane that resembles the place that they were programmed to believe in, their own personal version of hell or purgatory.

But even as these souls place themselves in these realms, their Spirit Guides or Guardian Angels will come into this place and assist them to move out of there and into the light. These spaces that were manifested are worthless. Souls are just wasting time and holding up their spiritual evolution. The Catholic faith claims that there is a place called "purgatory," but if you have been a part of that religion for forty years or so, then you would have seen that the rules on what purgatory is and who will go there have changed. In the 1960's the Catholic Church said it was a sin to set foot in any other church. Do you know how many interfaith weddings went unattended by parents because they were told that they would go to Hell if they were to be a part of anything that was not of the catholic faith?

If people would just be open to other ideas and spiritually educate themselves and use common sense, they would recognize that the truth has always been in front of them, the answers are right there. Just look inside yourself and ask the right questions. Man-made religion's rules always change. But God's universal laws are timeless and constant.

Q: So then what happens on judgment day if there is no Hell?

Traditional Western religion never gives you the whole picture. Judgment Day is such a negative term; it infers that we are going to be sentenced for our Earthy crimes. I refer to the process as a life review. We have a preview before we come to Earth, and we have a life review upon returning to our true home, Heaven.

While in the presence of God, the Masters, our Guardian Angels and our Spirit Guides, we are shown our entire life. We will reflect all our actions, thoughts, and deeds and how our soul interacted with others. We view opportunities that presented themselves to us and the different outcomes that we could have experienced had we taken those opportunities. We literally feel all of the emotional damage that we caused to others, and we also experience all of the love and the joy that we gave. So, when we are having that life review, we are very critical of ourselves. We judge ourselves without bias. No matter how many wonderful, good, and joyous things we have done, it is the negative that stands out in our mind more than the positive. We do this in life and after our physical life. We are our harshest critics. This is all of the punishment that is needed, an honest review of our life. Most souls stand before their council with heads hung low, weeping and ashamed of their earthy performance. Eventually, we learn from our life review so that we will not repeat certain negative experiences. Then we can choose to reincarnate again or study and learn lessons in the spirit world.

Q: *Is Lucifer the devil?*

Lucifer is the only dark angel that has been written about in the bible, and even that story hasn't been depicted correctly. In Heaven, he was the number one angel if you want to say, God's right hand. But there became a division in the heavens because Lucifer was very caught up in this planet and everything that was going on with humanity. He was studying the men of Earth and felt that they had something very special that the Angels did not, the gift of creation. Lucifer was envious of mankind's free will on this planet. Lucifer is a fallen Angel because he chose to leave Heaven so he could experience the astral levels and the Earth plane using free will to create whatever he wanted. The duality of Earth was very appealing. When he left heaven with God's permission, he took many Angels with him.

The agreement he made with God seemed like a good deal at the time. He would lose his high ranking and leave the Heavens. In return, he would gain the attribute of free will. He could create all that he desired. But during his decent to Earth he also encountered amnesia just like man does when he incarnates. So, Lucifer and his followers lost most of their memories of Heaven. They no longer had a clear recollection of where they came from, nor remembered the way back. All of the potential possibilities that he saw from heaven were faded memories. Because an Angel does not experience death, it is going to be a very long time before he can find his way back to the light.

This will happen only when God allows it.

So you can see, the Church's story of "The Fallen Angels" is quite different. They were not thrown out. They had a choice that God gave them. And no, Lucifer does not have a pointy tail or horns. This image was created to scare us.

Q: Then do you believe any of the bible?

Which Bible? I do believe that there is a great truth within all bibles, the Christian bible, the Catholic version, the Kabbala of Jewish Mysticism, the Koran which is the Islamic bible, Kitab-ul-Aqdas, the holy book of the Bahai and so on. But you must remember that the bible is something that you can take to five different people and receive five different interpretations for the same passage. Most importantly through the centuries, the Christian bible has been edited and translated several times. Through the translations of the languages, much of the true meaning was lost. A great deal of the original text was added to and taken away, and we only have bits and pieces of those stories. The truth is that men wrote all bibles, and much is left open to interpretation.

I believe that everything we need is within ourselves, the Christ consciousness. We just have to look within instead of reaching out. Whether it's addictions to shopping, chocolates, too much food or religious extremism, you know people are looking to fill that hole that is inside themselves. There is only one thing that can fill it up. That is a personal relationship with God and your unseen support team.

Q: Why is life on Earth so hard? There are many people who are having tremendous problems right now. Is there a reason for this?

Well we create a lot of the problems in our life. I always tell people, "If we wanted an easy route, then we would have stayed in Heaven." Life on Earth is not painless. That is why we chose to come here, to learn spiritual lessons from our Earthy experiences. At this particular time in our Earth's history, it is especially challenging for the collective consciousness as a whole. The energy and people's thoughts are more negative than positive, so this has an effect on everyone. It is the current state of affairs that our Earth is in; everything is a reflection of us. We mirror and reflect our issues onto others so we have to deal with them. So that is why it is important that everyone individually take responsibility and work on improving his or her spiritual life. Once you realize that everything that you do, think, and say really matters, and it affects the whole population, then you have taken responsibility for your part of creating the world that we live in. What you do today and tomorrow creates the future. It affects not just you personally but the entire world.

But most of our individual problems in this life we create, whether we chose it before we came in or whether we are just making them up as we go along, we're creating our reality. So the more that you buy into negative thought patterns, "Life is Harsh," "Something Bad is going to Happen," then you will create exactly what you have prepared for. We humans love to dwell on the negative when we could just as easily dwell on the good and the positive.

*It should be our principal business
to conquer ourselves and,
from day to day, to go on increasing
in strength and perfection.
Above all, however, it is necessary for
us to strive to conquer our little
temptations, such as fits of anger,
suspicions, jealousies, envy,
deceitfulness, vanity, attachments,
and evil thoughts.
For in this way we shall acquire
strength to subdue greater ones.*

- St. Francis de Sales

CHAPTER

11

TWENTY QUESTIONS

*A*s I travel across the country, I am asked many spiritual questions. I have included the twenty most frequently asked questions by the public from TV, radio, and lectures.

1. Who is GOD?

Human beings like to label and categorize everything, so God is a concept that is hard for the intellectual mind to grasp. Father, Mother, God is the creator of all that is. God is a part of everything that is manifested. Humans are all sparks of the creator of God. We emanate that light because God created us, and we are fragments of the collective consciousness, which is the Godhead.

2. Why do we have so many religions on this planet, each claiming that they are God's chosen?

Religions were created by man, for men that are at different levels of spiritual consciousness. The ancient prophets were men who used their minds as a filter when they channeled information. Each man's interpretation was a bit different because his belief system colored the information as it was received. There is a core of truth that still runs through every religion. That truth is unconditional love. God does not have a favorite race or religion. He loves us all equally, saints and sinners. Organized religion is only an Earthly concept. In Heaven, there is no religion; there is only love.

3. Why are western organized religions so insistent that the Bible has never been changed?

Organized religions are fearful that they will lose control and the financial support of their followers if the truth is openly revealed. When the bible was first put together in 4 AD, it was censored. Some books written by prophets were accepted; others were disregarded. Through the western translations from language to language, much of the original meaning and the intent had been changed. There are words in the original Aramaic text that have no substitutes in the English language. The bible originates from sacred scrolls, but King James edited the bible, and in modern day, there are many interpretations, such as The New Living Bible to the Saint Joseph version.

4. What part do the Dead Sea scrolls play in religion?

The Dead Sea scrolls are ancient sacred texts that were discovered in 1946. Most were fragments, but one scroll was intact. I believe that they are the original texts from which our modern day bible stems. These scrolls and fragments once translated will be the key to lost information and prophecy that have significant meaning for mankind today. This ancient knowledge has the ability to set people free from their self-imposed limitations, whether that limitation is man-made religion, belief in reincarnation, or that we co-create our life with God.

5. Why do some people pray to saints?

Saints are highly evolved spiritual beings that man has recognized and labeled. I believe that many of the Saints are highly evolved because of their many successful Earthly incarnations. Their last life on Earth was about sacrificing and doing good works for humanity. They were key players in many people's lives. They set an example.

I believe that many Saints stay true to their spiritual form in the spirit world, and they continue their work by assisting us from the other side by answering prayers and by being the vehicle for miracles and healings.

Saints, Angels, and Spirit Guides are all helpers to God. They petition God on our behalf. No prayer can be fulfilled without God's stamp of approval.

6. What is the difference between a psychic, a channel, and a Medium?

First, I'd like to clarify that people who work as psychics, channels, or mediums all have different levels of skills and abilities. Even some who claim that they have these abilities are frauds. So, some skepticism is healthy. Before you consider spending your hard earned money, I would suggest that you know something about them. Does their information ring true for you, and are they living their truth? Are they in their integrity?

A psychic has the ability to tune into a person's energy, aura, or an object and receive information. A medium has the ability to contact departed loved ones and spirits on the other side. These spirits communicate telepathically through feelings and pictures. This is a rare gift, and all psychics are not mediums.

Channeling is the ability to relay messages and teachings from the highest level of consciousness to gain knowledge for personal growth to improve the quality of our lives. When channeling information from the universe, the person who is the instrument must raise his or her vibration to interface with the high frequencies of spirit.

7.What is a premonition?

A premonition is foreknowledge of a future event. A premonition can manifest as a dream or a vision. It is often associated when a person is given information in the dream state that reveals a future event that has to do with a person or place. The event will come to pass in the way that the person was shown before it actually happened. The premonition will be confirmed as the vision plays itself out. A person is shown the future by "spirit"; therefore, they know it to be a true foretelling of an event to come.

8.How many times can a soul reincarnate?

Some of us will reincarnate hundreds of times, some thousands, and others only a few. It depends on what the individual soul chooses for its growth process. There are souls that come to Earth and find it much too difficult here because this is one of the most challenging and most taxing places in which to learn. They chose to evolve at a slower rate in the heavens. If a soul chooses never to incarnate on this planet again, it is not forced to. Others return as soon as possible;

they are eager to learn lessons. There is no limit.

9. What is a twin soul?

A twin soul is the other half of you. In the Heavens, a small amount of very evolved souls will choose to divide their energy and incarnate in two different bodies, in two different parts of the world. They will cram two totally different experiences into the same period of time on Earth. They do this to quickly evolve and work out many karmic debts or just to experience a very special event on Earth from two different perspectives.

Many more souls are here now in this new millennium to experience a special event in the Earth's history called the ascension. In the ascension, humanity, the collective consciousness, humans, and the Earth have the ability to go into the light at the same time.

10. What is enlightenment?

True enlightenment is a state of being. It is a state of knowingness by mastering unconditional love and grace twenty-four hours a day, every day, while still in the physical body. When you live in this state of being, it is impossible to allow anyone to push your buttons. You come from love no matter what is said or done.

Enlightened masters see the intent and the lessons behind others' actions. They take nothing personally.

They have the ability to raise their vibration to overcome their physical limitations, which are illusions to survive. They have the ability to exist by eating very little or nothing at all. When people eat nothing, they are called breatharians. They can also circumvent dying a physical death and chose to walk over and disappear into the next dimension.

11. What is happening to our food sources?

Our environment and our food sources have been and continue to be contaminated. In most cities, the water is unsafe from bacteria and pollutants and the large amount of chlorine used to kill bacteria. It is very important to drink clean water, spring water, not the city faucet water that they are trying to kill us with.

People who eat red meat, chicken, and dairy do so at a risk. If you really saw what you were eating, I don't think you would eat it. The animals are pumped full of chemicals, antibiotics, steroids, and too much estrogen. This is then passed onto to the human that consumes the animal or the dairy product. Organic everything is the best way to eat.

It is also very important that we replace the nutrients that our diet is lacking with natural supplements and try to eat as healthy as we can. We need to take an interest in educating ourselves on what we are ingesting.

12. What is a dream?

Dreamtime is your doorway into the spirit world. When the body goes to sleep, our soul is set free. During the dream state the soul travels. We visit other dimensions, travel to check up on people that we love, and communicate with loved ones on the other side. We do many things. As we awake, our subconscious mind filters our memories of our dreamtime activities, and we mostly remember bits and pieces.

13. Is it possible to knowingly participate in our dreamtime journeys?

Many people take time to reprogram their subconscious mind to help them remember their dreams. The next step would be to learn the art of astral travel. This is the ability to consciously will your soul to a destination and actively participate in lighter body travel.

14. What can an ordinary person do to make a difference in this world?

I would like to be so brave as to ask that each human being to weigh his or her actions and assess what the end results will be. We need to look at our actions from an unbiased point of view, and then maybe we might understand that person or situation better and learn what is in the best interest for all concerned. I would ask all of the people of the world to take each individual in your life and love him or her like you would a newborn child. Give more of yourself whether it is money, love or even your time that's so precious. Be a great friend, business associate, family member, and humanitarian. Lend a helping hand when you can even if that means that it is a sacrifice. Love is the key to all things. How would the world change if everyone took this step? We would have a positive, loving, balanced world for all to live in.

15. Do you believe that there is life on other planets?

Yes, many planets in this solar system, as well as others, sustain life. It would be presumptuous of us to think we were the only beings that God created.

16. Are Ghosts real?

Yes, ghosts are as real as everything on earth. But unlike humans, their energy has become ethereal, which is a lighter body. They are in the next realm that is parallel to ours. At times ghosts and humans coexist together sharing different spaces and places on this earth.

17. What is soul retrieval work?

Soul retrieval work is designed to help souls who are confused at the time of their physical death to cross over into the spirit world. This work is also done to try and reach ghosts and help them find their way as well. Soul retrieval is done by many different spirits in the heavens. They do this by approaching the lost soul through communication and the shifting of that soul's consciousness. Humans here on Earth can also do soul retrieval work during the dreamtime when they are able to astral travel.

18. What is Karma?

Karma is the universal law of cause and effect. For every action, there is a reaction. There is both positive and negative Karma, which must be kept in balance based on our choices. If we incur a karmic debt, then it must be paid back. For example, if you were to murder someone in this life, then, eventually, you too would have another life together in which you would be able to pay back that Karma, perhaps by being their caregiver or maybe by sacrificing yourself for them in some way, thus burning the karmic tie.

19. Are there karmic ties between mankind and nature?

Yes, as man creates karma between two individual human souls, man can also be indebted to a different group of God's children like the animal kingdom. If you abuse the planet and create a karmic debt from that abuse, then perhaps in your next life you will devote yourself to environmental issues such as saving the rainforest or being a caretaker to an endangered species. This is an example of group karma

20. Are we approaching the end of the world?

As we enter this new millennium and continue to allow mass destruction, the planet cleanses herself through different Earth changes in order to heal. This will not be the "end" of the world, but the world population will be drastically reduced, and we will continue to suffer collectively as long as we continue our negative actions. Mother earth will birth a lighter version of herself thus completing the ascension. For those who do not make the ascension and refuse to grow spiritually, they will be able to start their evolution over on the lower denser version of Earth.

SPIRITUAL TERMS

Akashic Records

Sometimes called the book of life. A record kept by each soul that includes words spoken, deeds and thoughts. This is an eternal record of every experience and life the soul encounters.

Arch Angels

Angels of the highest order, they are the Angels closest to God.

Ascension

Sometimes called the graduation. It is a shift in mankind and in Mother Earth's consciousness and their frequency going into a higher realm.

Aura

The colorful electro-magnetic field that radiates from and around a physical body. Sometimes referred to as the 'over-soul', it is the part of the soul that can be seen with the eye.

Blueprint

Is a human souls map, which was created before we ever came into a life or incarnation. An outline of our live plan that we predetermine in the spirit world to fulfill spiritual contracts, and karmic debts.

Blue Ray Children

Highly evolved spiritual children that represent the next evolutionary stage of mankind. Sometimes called Indigo Children.

Chakra

The human body has seven energy centers called Chakras. A psychic can see these colorful energy centers in a persons aura or spiritual body. The spiritual energy centers are directly linked to the physical health of the human body. When in perfect working order they are seen as bright vibrant vortexes of energy.

Channel

A person who has the ability to access the universal consciousness and translate information from the cosmos or from spirits.

Clairaudiance

The ability to hear sounds from the Spirit realm

Clairvoyance

The ability to clearly see spirits or symbols and relay the information.

Deja Vu

A soul memory recall of a familiar place or person from a past life. A past life event memory.

A current event that evokes a memory of the event happening before. A memory that has taken place in the spiritual plane that is now taking place in the physical realm.

Earth's Cleansing

Mother Earth is purging of all the negativity on the planet. The cleansing is manifesting physically through earth changes such as sever storms, fires, flooding, volcanoes, and earthquakes.

Ego

Our conscious mind that passes judgement and makes decisions based on appearances or intelligence.

Guardian Angels

Two specific Angels are assigned to each of us. They never leave us from our birth, they help and protect us during our life and continue with us through the transformation we call death and into the afterlife.

God

The Supreme Being, the source of everything, the Universal Consciousness, the one creator of all that is.

God-part-self

Our higher consciousness, the part of the soul that is connected to God and that is perfect.

Karma

The Universal Law of cause and effect. What you sow, so you shall reap. Every action causes a reaction.

Kundalini Energy

Is the sexual and spiritual energy that is associated with the source of our life energy. Kundalini energy is stored in our root chakra or the energy center at the base of the spine. Kundalini energy is sometimes referred to as the fire within.

Master Spirit Guide

A highly evolved and trained Spirit Guide that aides humanity and helps to teach younger Spirits Guides.

Medium

A person who has the ability to communicate with the otherside: departed loved ones, Angels, and Spirit Guides and other souls residing in the spirit world.

Near Death Experience

When the physical body experiences death and the soul leaves the body, travels to the spirit realm and then returns to the body with the remembrance of the experience.

Psychic

A person who has the ability to 'read' another persons energy or vibrations and relay accurate information about their past, present and future.

Psychic Empathy

The ability to feel the emotions and physical sensations of another, either a spirit or of a human.

Psychometry

The ability to 'read' objects or photos by tuning into

the vibration or energy field surrounding that object and receiving information about it.

Reincarnation

The rebirth of a soul into a new body.

Silver Cord

The etheric cord that attaches the physical body to the spiritual body, the soul.

Soul

The spirit, the essence, or core of our being that is eternal.

Spirit Guide

A spirit that helps us with a specific aspect of our spiritual development while on Earth. We each have one Spirit Guide that stays with us from birth through death. Other Sprit Guides are assigned to us for different periods of time to help us through different phases of life.

Spiritual Reading

A personal counseling session with a Psychic Medium whom chooses to receive information only from God and his helpers.

Subconscious

A part of the mind that holds all memories. The subconscious mind acts as a filter for the conscious mind.

Telepathy

The ability to send and receive thoughts as a way of communicating with others.

The Council

A highly evolved group of twelve Ascended Masters, sometimes referred to as 'The Elders'. They are in charge of humanity's Karma. The Council is in charge of 'The Book of Life'.

Universal Intelligence

The mind of God. Sometimes called universal conscience.

Victim Soul

A person who has chosen to soak up a large amount of Karma for humanity.

TESTIMONIALS & APPRECIATION

Being a messenger is not always easy. Yes, there are those who come to me looking for confirmation that they are on the right track and those who are living a fulfilling, joyful life. But more often than not, people seek me out for solutions to life's most difficult problems. Since I began my spiritual counseling work, I always forewarn those who come to me. I do not edit the information that is given. Spirit is kind in the delivery, but direct solutions are the sometimes hardest to apply to our lives. Humans find that change is difficult, but to improve our lives, change is usually in our best interest. There is no magic pill that will sort out our problems for us. We create our future.

For those who want to hear a candy coated version of their issues, I am not the counselor that they should see. I have not been given this gift to relay half-truths or delete information at my leisure. My mission is to truly help those who want answers.

So when I receive a note of thanks or a confirmation from a client who took action on the suggestions that "spirit" put before him or her, I receive personal satisfaction because that person faced their challenges and made improvements in their life. This bravery motivates me to keep moving forward.

I am honored to play a small role in healing lives, and I give thanks to "the Great Spirit" for allowing me be used as his messenger.

Dear Michelle,

I just wanted to thank you so much for being a guest on our radio morning show here in Alabama this past Tuesday. Not only were you an interesting guest, you may have saved my life.

While we laughed on air, you relayed that I am a "Cyst Maker" and in need of a female exam. I scheduled an appointment the moment I got off the air with you. The truth is that I had not been to a GYN in many years. The doctor examined me this morning...only to reveal I have a large growth in my uterus. My sonogram is scheduled this Monday to determine it's severity.

My point is...I would have not made that appointment had it not been for you! I have over 100 thousand listeners in my morning show audience...and you would not believe the phone calls I had after your interview. A neighbor, whom I have never met, left cookies and a note on my door ....saying I was in her prayers...and that with God's Love all things were possible!

I am not overly concerned about these medical problems...just want to gain fast treatment. But I thought you should know how much I appreciate you. You are an amazing woman!

Sincerely,
Jessica,
Morning Show Host

Dear Michelle,

I would like to thank you from the bottom of my heart for your graciousness in donating your valuable time to me during a private reading over the phone. You told me so many things that were absolutely right! I am appreciative and happy that I took your advice about not having major back surgery. I have been doing an alternative therapy for over a year now and it has helped my body tremendously. I still have those painful times, but they are far and few between now. I was hesitant at first but I talked it over with a medical professional and he helped me to realize that it is my body and I had every right to cancel the operation, so I did. I am very grateful.

I play the tape recording of my reading over and over, as there is such an abundance of valuable information that your spirit guides gave me. I have started the process of eliminating certain obstacles, it has been a slow process but your guidance has opened my mind, body, and spirit in a positive direction.

God has truly blessed you with a beautiful gift to help those that you meet and I value the fact that your blessing touched my life. You are truly an Angel on Earth.

Sincerely Yours,
Margaret in OR

Michelle,

Regina and I met you while you were touring Dallas for book signings. You had told us to expect a baby and he would be an Indigo child. We officially found out just before Christmas that we are going to have a baby. Thank you, he is a dream come true.

Thanks,
Clint & Regina, TX

Dear Michelle: Thank you for the interview you just recently did on our morning Radio show. This will be a day that will be forever remembered by myself. I was overwhelmed by the information you shared with me about my father. It made me speechless and I apologize. The words you shared had been confirmed by other members of my family. I have a feeling of closure on questions that have been lingering in my heart for 25 years. I thank God for people like yourself that can help comfort a grieving family and help give some encouragement in trying times.

Thank You
Kevin,
AM Radio Personality in IL

Michelle -

Thanks so much for the radio interview with us this morning.......we'd LOVE to have you back this week for listeners.

I was very impressed (and a little shocked) by your reading. It was very accurate. Thanks & we look forward to talking to you again soon!

Stephanie
AM Radio Personality in MI

Dear Michelle,

What an amazing intuitive you are! The reading that you did for my husband was incredible! You were extremely accurate and for the most part brave to give all information as you received it. As a result of his reading, John changed his profession, made a variety of changes in his personal life and today is a much more contented individual.

Before long and after careful consideration, I decided to have a "phone reading" This was a tough decision for me to make - I always figured you had to be in the same room with the psychic to have a thriving and accurate reading. I can't begin to explain to you how precise you were with my reading. I can only assume that you are truly a brilliant human being.

I had sent some photos and made a list of questions for myself to ask you - just as you had suggested. All the details you gave me during my reading were amazing! You told me about things that only my physician, husband and veterinarian would have known about. You knew personal things that I had not shared with anyone about my son. You knew unusual things about the passing of my beloved pet, Bandit. You filled my soul with bliss, my heart with passion, and my eyes with tears - you are truly an exceptional individual.

I often wonder if people do in fact appreciate a supreme clairvoyant like you. Thank you for all the energy you put into our readings. Thank you for sharing your talents with us mortals.

Wishing you abundant peace, blessing, prosperity, and heaps of love,

Brenda in GA

Hello Michelle

First, let me say that we have interviewed many, many fine and interesting people on our radio show. Out of all that we have interviewed, I think that you where the most charming, most interesting and above all, the one special person, with the most ever, listener response. Also, I might add that you are the only one we have ever asked back. We where thrilled when you accepted our invitation.

I cannot begin to tell you the MAJOR impact you had on my friend. The uncanny accuracy, that only he and his sister and mother would know, on his dad's untimely death. After the show he broke down with joy.

Michelle we wait excitedly for the next interview.

Thanks again
Sincerely your friend,
Bob (Guitarman) Jackson
WRXX 95.3

"Michelle Whitedove held the listening audience captive during the entire half-hour segment!"
"Listener's were shocked to hear the accuracy of her readings" "We were overwhelmed with response on the phones and look forward to our next segment with Michelle!!"

The Mix Morning Cafe w/ Vanceman & Biscuit
Mix 96 Fm WKOV / Jackson, Ohio
Bryan Vance- Host / Program Director

"Michelle Whitedove is a very gifted and blessed person who proved to me beyond a shadow of a doubt, when during a show Michelle actually reached and communicated with those who have passed and are now on "The Other Side" .
What an experience!"
Rob McConnell, Television Personality - Canada

Michelle,

Thank you for the interesting evening at our local New Age bookstore. You are so enchanting and fascinating. I found your lecture to be not only sensational, but inspiring. You gave me a message from my late husband, to warn my son about something specific. Saturday I called my son, James and relayed the message. He said he was in a quandary about a business deal that he had agreed to do. Later in the week he found out that the people with the business deal were not on the up and up.

I thank you again, it would have been a financial disaster.
Thanks. -
Cindy in Miami

Hello Michelle,

I attended your lecture at Liberties Bookstore. At that time my lady friend's son in law, age 39, had recently been diagnosed with melanoma. You allowed us one question. I asked how much time did Todd have. You thought for a minute and answered, "August." At the time I thought you meant Aug, 2000, and I passed the information to my girlfriend, Norma. She snapped, "Why did you tell me that?" I told her it was for her to prepare herself.

When Aug 2000 passed without his passing over, she gradually began to see the blessing in your message, as he slowly began his physical descent. She spent the past three weeks with him and her daughter, in Oklahoma City. He declined rapidly until the last week spent in coma, and finally drew his last breath at 8 AM Friday, 8/3/01. The night before, she had spoken to him alone, telling him he had gone through enough, and it was time for him to let go and be assured that his wife and son would be ok. Norma was better prepared for his crossing than her daughter, and the other family members, thanks to your message given to me on May 24, 2000. She will now be a light for someone else in similar circumstances. I thought you might want to know how your courage in revealing the month of Todd's crossing gave Norma the courage to make her vigil with Todd.

May you continue to be a light for others.

Blessings,

Jack - Pompano Beach, FL

Dear Michelle,

I don't know if you'll remember me but I had a very disturbing reading with you in April concerning my son and daughter-in-law, during which you relayed great concerns for our families safety.

Although I appeared calm during the reading, I was trembling inside and left with the concerns and warnings you gave me. I then had to convey them to my husband (who is not enlightened to say the least) and my daughter and future son-in-law. Had it not been for your tape recording where you described our daughter-in-law in such minute detail, I would never have gotten through to any of them. They, too, recognized your clear description of the daughter-in-law and were at a loss about what to do. You warned me that she had been scheming to get family assets in her name as well as life insurance policies.

I am usually a very sensitive person, yet I had this evil being married to my son who was now plotting my family's murder. I had to choose between my family's immediate safety and following your suggestion on getting some documentation on this girl. This was a nightmare that I could not believe was happening: How could I have not seen and felt the evil in this girl.

Additionally, we were only visiting Florida for a short time and the daughter-in-law was coming in to the funds for the sale of her home, which I was to be Trustee for her. The girl continued to escalate her poor behavior and actually showed her hand by raising a fist against our son in the presence of several family members. After we discussed the protection of the family issues with our son, he revealed that she had threatened to stab him, on several occasions.

We then questioned our son if he wanted to remain in the relationship and he said no he was stressed out from her and wanted to leave. I called her attorney and declined the Trustee and told him that they were not getting along and that my son was seeking a divorce.

Now, as you had stated, her new attorney is coming after our son for an incident that she caused.

I GREATLY APPRECIATE your prayers. Even though my reading was shocking, thank you for the warning. We have removed this threat from our family.

Karen in VA

Dear Michelle Whitedove,   May 2002

I met you several years ago, around 1998 at the Magical Forest Bookstore where you were giving a lecture. I came to see because I had heard that you were incredibly gifted. Anyway, after the lecture you started giving personal messages but I felt you had become too aggressive with me and I walked out, I was full of anger.

Not only is this email an apology...it is also a Thank You. Michelle, on that day... You actually SAVED MY LIFE.

Let me explain. I had been going through a terrible period in my life and at the time had been diagnosed with the illness Hepatitis C. I was actually taking an experimental medication for my condition along with popping prescribed medication for depression. All the while I was drinking alcohol because couldn't find the strength to cope with my medical problems and the difficulties of raising teenagers.

You could clearly see what I was doing, I was really a mess and you didn't hesitate to call me on my issues, although I didn't want to hear it. When you mentioned my LIVER and I was stunned. You told me it "wasn't my time to leave this world" but that I was headed toward death if I didn't "stop the medication." You continued... but by the time I left the store, I was flabbergasted and as I said quite upset. Even still, I did listen to your advice and stopped the medication and drinking.

Your message never really left my mind and had came back to me many times until I finally got myself together. I would like to apologize to you for my misguided anger and to thank you from the bottom of my heart for that message. Yes, you were aggressive but I believe that your spirit guides wanted you to be...for my own sake. I am now aware that when one goes to a psychic-medium, one does not always get the information one wants to hear. Thank you for your direct honesty.

Since that time, I have come through major life changes and am very well, in both my mind and body. I have been using holistic treatments and I've 'found myself' all over again through a strong connection to spirit and even learned how to tap into some of my own intuitive abilities.

Why am I telling you all this today, after all this time? Well, this morning when I was cleaning out some boxes full of papers I "accidentally" came across one of your flyers. I saw it as a sign to get this message to you, make my peace and thank you. I hope this message finds you happy and well and with an abundance of Love.

Peace to you in Divine Light.
Sydney

May 18, 2002
Dear Michelle:

I will always be grateful for your kindness, openness, willingness to share your very special gifts with me and the rest of the world.

For years, I've had a lot of problems with my female organs including pain, irregular bleeding and constant nausea. I saw three doctors who could not find anything wrong, my ultrasounds were normal, as well as all the blood tests and exams.

When I went to see you, you urged me to see a doctor, you said that my uterus looked like it had an abnormal shape and that I had endometriosis. You also said that I needed to have surgery as soon as possible, the doctor would have to fix or remove my left fallopian tube and he would find other things such as a growth or other unexpected problems but that he would be able to fix them and that the surgery would be a success.

Because of your insistence, I made an appointment with a well known fertility doctor. He confirmed that my left fallopian tube was in very bad shape, however, the uterus seem to be ok and no other problems were expected. He was almost certain that I didn't have endometriosis.

I had surgery soon after, and during surgery the doctor found that due to some scar tissue, my uterus was attached in the bottom back to the bowel, deforming the uterus and giving it an irregular shape. They were not able to see this in ultrasounds because of the location of the deformity. The doctor was able to remove the scar tissue and correct this problem, allowing for my uterus to return to it's normal shape.

The left fallopian tube was in such bad shape and it had to be removed. The doctor also found two growths, one on the bladder and another on the uterus, which he was not expecting to find just as you predicted. He was also surprised to find that there were some spots with endometriosis.

Everything went well during the surgery, the doctor used lasers to remove the endometriosis and the growths, which turned out to be benign.

You told me that once I had the surgery, the overall feeling of tiredness and nausea that I have had for years would go away and that I was going to feel well again. It has been almost three weeks after my surgery and I have not felt this good in years. I am not nauseous anymore, I don't have any pain and I don't feel tired. I can't remember the last time I felt this good.

Earlier this week I went to the doctor for the surgery follow-up visit and everything looks great. He told me that without the surgery I was running a very high risk of having a serious problem that would result in infertility, internal bleeding, and possibly the need for emergency surgery, just as you warned me.

I am very thankful for all your advice and your vision into my health problems.

With love,

Marina

Dear Michelle   **5-13-02**

Words could never come close to expressing the feelings of peace and incredible love that accompanied me home on Saturday after our private reading. It will be one year since my partner passed away to join his loved one's on the other side. This year has been incredibly painful for me with many questions that surrounded his death. Your reading was incredibly on target. You were able to totally recapture my partner's very essence and love of life. More importantly, for this first time since his passing, you were able to bring a sense of closure to me on many fronts. Your wisdom regarding on my health and my Dad's was accurate too.

I will make every attempt to move on, as best I can - but please be sure of one thing - your talent and God given gift, has given me a reason to move on, to make my time on Earth as meaningful and as loving as possible, while at the same time knowing that my partner will be forever watching over me and guiding me through life from a very special place just beyond my reach.

Thank you again, In peace and love
Ric

*The virtue of angels is that
they cannot deteriorate;
their flaw is that they
cannot improve.
Man's flaw is that
he can deteriorate;
and his virtue is that
he can improve.*

– The Talmud

Prayer of Thanks

We return thanks to our mother,
the earth, which sustains us.
We return thanks to the rivers and
streams, which supply us with water.
We return thanks to all herbs,
which furnish medicines for
the cure of our diseases.
We return thanks to the moon and
stars, which have given us their light
when the sun was gone.
We return thanks to the sun, that has
looked upon the earth with a
beneficent eye.
Lastly, we return thanks to the
Great Spirit, in Whom is embodied all
goodness, and Who directs all things
for the good of Her children.

Iroquois Prayer, adapted

Michelle Whitedove is a renowned Psychic - Medium and Channel who is currently the host of her own "Spiritual TV Talk Show". She conducts private counseling sessions, teaches spiritual development courses, and lectures across the country where she uses her gifts to relay conversations from the Spirit World to those in the physical world. Michelle has been featured on PBS television and has done numerous interviews in America as well as Europe.

For more information and a list of public appearances Go to: www.MichelleWhitedove.com

To order additional copies of this book call 800-444-2524

Angels Are Talking